Social Psychology

FOUNDATIONS OF MODERN PSYCHOLOGY SERIES

Richard S. Lazarus, Editor

WILLIAM W. LAMBERT

Professor of Psychology, Sociology, and Anthropology
Cornell University

WALLACE E. LAMBERT

Professor of Psychology
McGill University

second edition

Social Psychology

PRENTICE-HALL, INC., ENGLEWOOD CLIFFS, NEW JERSEY

Library of Congress Cataloging in Publication Data

LAMBERT, WILLIAM WILSON
   Social psychology

  (Foundations of modern psychology series)
  Bibliography: p.
  1. Social psychology—Addresses, essays, lectures.
  I. Lambert, Wallace E., joint author. II. Title.
HM251.L23 1973   301.1   72–13930
ISBN 0–13–818021–0
ISBN 0–13–818013–X (pbk)

10 9 8 7 6 5 4 3 2 1

Prentice-Hall International, Inc., London

Prentice-Hall of Australia, Pty. Ltd., Sydney

Prentice-Hall of Canada, Ltd., Toronto

Prentice-Hall of India Private Limited, New Delhi

Prentice-Hall of Japan, Inc., Tokyo

*Picture credits: cartoons are reprinted by permission of Mrs. H. T. Webster; photo-
graphs are from* Ces Visages Qui Sont Un Pays *by the National Film Board of Canada,*
1967.

In memory of Harry Brown Lambert

Contents

ix

SIX

SEVEN

Foundations of
Modern Psychology Series

The tremendous growth and vitality of psychology and its increasing fusion with the social and biological sciences demand a search for new approaches to teaching at the introductory level. We can no longer feel content with the traditional basic course, geared as it usually is to a single text that tries to skim everything, that sacrifices depth for breadth. Psychology has become too diverse for any one person, or group, to write about with complete authority. The alternative, a book that ignores many essential areas in order to present more comprehensively and effectively a particular aspect or view of psychology, is also insufficient, for in this solution many key areas are simply not communicated to the student at all.

The Foundations of Modern Psychology Series was the first in what has become a growing trend in psychology toward groups of short texts dealing with various basic subjects, each written by an active authority. It was conceived with the idea of providing greater flexibility for instructors teaching general courses than was ordinarily available in the large, encyclopedic textbooks, and greater depth of presentation for individual topics not typically given much space in introductory textbooks.

The earliest volumes appeared in 1963, the latest not until 1973. Well over one and a quarter million copies, collectively, have been sold, attesting to the widespread use of these books in the teaching of psychology. Individual volumes have been used as supplementary texts, or as *the* text, in various undergraduate courses in psychology, education, public health, and sociology, and clusters of volumes have served as the text in beginning undergraduate courses in general psychology. Groups of volumes have been translated into eight languages, including Dutch, Hebrew, Italian, Japanese, Polish, Portuguese, Spanish, and Swedish.

With wide variation in publication date and type of content, some of the volumes need revision, while others do not. We have left this decision to the individual author who best knows his book in relation to the state of the field. Some will remain unchanged, some will be modestly changed, and still others completely rewritten. In the new series edition, we have also opted for some variation in the length and style of individual books, to reflect the different ways in which they have been used as texts.

There has never been stronger interest in good teaching in our colleges and universities than there is now; and for this the availability of high quality, well-written, and stimulating text materials highlighting the exciting and continuing search for knowledge is a prime prerequisite. This is especially the case in undergraduate courses where large numbers of students must have access to suitable readings. The Foundations of Modern Psychology Series represents our ongoing attempt to provide college teachers with the best textbook materials we can create.

Richard S. Lazarus

Social Psychology

Social Psychology, Its Major Concerns and Approaches

Social psychology is the study of individuals in their social and cultural settings. Through training and experience, the social psychologist learns to raise his sights from strictly psychological concerns and to include in his perspective the social world that influences how people think, feel, behave, and interact. With this broad perspective, the social psychologist becomes sensitive to the ways in which psychological processes are colored by the many social influences that contribute to the development and ultimate style of human personalities. Because he is interested in social and cultural settings for behavior as well as in individuals, he makes observations and conducts experiments with both social context and individual in mind, controlling, where possible, the influence of social context or of personality to better understand how they interact in normal situations.

Some social experiences, however, are unique, tied to particular moments; others recur and follow a pattern with common causes or effects. It is to these *recurring* processes that social psychologists turn, and it is largely to increase our understanding of these processes that social psychologists experiment, construct theories, and develop methods of measurement. Consider, for example, the acquaintance proc-

LOVE AT FIRST SIGHT

© 1937 N.Y.TRIBUNE INC.

The acquaintance process

ess as two persons meet for the first time. Human beings have long been interested in this recurring social event and Professor Theodore Newcomb at the University of Michigan conducted an extended experimental study of it.[1] Becoming acquainted is a far more complex process than we may think at first, as we shall see in Chapter 5. One of the reasons it is complex and difficult to observe is that it depends so much on what goes on within the two persons involved—the particular motives and wishes, the personality traits, attitudes, and learnings from the past that they bring with them, and the accurate and inaccurate information they receive from and about one another. No one who wants to describe and experiment with the acquaintance process can ignore such inner states. In fact, the habits, attitudes, per-

[1] T. M. Newcomb, *The Acquaintance Process* (New York: Holt, Rinehart & Winston, 1961). (Selected references are given so that the interested reader can turn to more extensive treatments of important topics.)

ceptions, judgments, and motivations of each participant make the acquaintance process possible and give it a particular style. At the same time, these personal factors are themselves modified through the process of social interaction. The social psychologist is particularly skilled at describing and explaining both the psychological effects of social contact and the social process itself. For example, by standardizing the social contexts in which acquaintance takes place, he can explore individual differences in reacting to this form of social interaction, and by observing large numbers of unacquainted individuals in various social contexts, he can examine the general nature of the acquaintance process itself.

So social psychology leans on other branches of psychology. But this is not the end of the story because the concerns of social psychologists are of interest to all behavioral scientists, even to historians. Sociologists, for instance, have played a particularly active part in developing our discipline, since recurring processes like becoming acquainted also depend on social rules and structures for their occurrence and facilitation. For instance, it is particularly rare and difficult for the low man in a social order to become acquainted with the top man. To study the social situation in detail, we must know about and be able to use the theories and measures provided by sociologists. Social psychology is indeed often referred to as "micro-sociology" or "micro-anthropology" since the analyst must lower his sights from the larger problems of these disciplines to see the finer texture of person-to-person relationships—the converse of raising his sights to include more than the usual concerns of psychology.

Social psychology is, then, a meeting place of many interests, ideas, and facts. Since World War II, the discipline has grown greatly until now it is one of the lustiest children in the behavioral science family. It is a boastful and raucous child, possibly because it has so many parents. And it has its growing pains that sometimes result in a messiness and disarray of facts and theories; but one can view the disarray as a sign of creativity, and the boastfulness as a preliminary step to self-confidence. At any rate, we shall assume that such is the case in this book. Despite the growing pains, since the mid-sixties the field of social psychology has become of focal interest to young people around the world who are anxious to change and improve established and time-honored ways of life and patterns of values. In certain respects social psychology has shown its immaturity as a reference discipline at the same time that it has gained recognition as one of the few available guides for making rational changes in societies and in people. As we shall see, social psychology is now based as much in community and interpersonal settings as it is in university laboratories.

Many of the recurring processes that social psychologists have turned their attention to are the very ones that supposedly already are explained by common sense. When common-sense notions become part of one's everyday language, they are accepted by many as wisdom and are often used as principles for action or codes of conduct. Naive notions such as "Man is basically selfish" or "The more you get to know someone, the more you like him" are now challenged by social psychologists who ask these questions: "How do these codes work their way into the very structure of our language?" "To what extent do we act or judge on the basis of such notions?" "Are they valid?" It is at this point of challenge that the excitement of modern social psychology can be acutely felt, and it is largely in this century that the general critical tenor of Western thought has reached into the realm of social psychology with a serious intent to awaken us from our dogmatic slumbers regarding the social nature of man. Social psychology plays an important role in human affairs by developing methods and criteria for discovering what our common-sense—or even our more sophisticated—notions about interpersonal behavior actually are, and for checking their validity.

When we view the extreme variations in the interpretations of man's social nature that have appeared over the ages, we realize how great a need there is to check on their validity. Through the past centuries, various thinkers have assumed, for example, that man is perfectly rational, totally irrational; largely kind, rootedly cruel; especially aggressive, basically benign; a creature of wishful illusion, a purveyor of valid insight into the nature of things. What is intriguing about these doctrines is that each was put forth by otherwise profound and reasonable people as a sufficient explanation of man's complex social nature. Apparently the social philosophers who proposed them were in search of what Gordon Allport of Harvard University has called "a simple and sovereign" doctrine on the social nature of man; that is, a type of philosophical Ohm's law that would be as simple but yet as general as possible.[2] These doctrines have left their mark on everyday language and each has its ardent proponents today. University students, in fact, are fascinated nowadays by surveying all that is known about man's egoistic or altruistic inclinations. Many see the contemporary relevance of Hobbes's and LeDantec's views of man's egoism, especially since one can follow the course of the debate right up to the present as social psychologists examine and measure individual and cultural differences in helping behavior, Machiavellianism, or achieve-

[2] G. W. Allport, "The Historical Background of Modern Social Psychology," in *Handbook of Social Psychology,* ed. G. Lindzey (Reading, Mass.: Addison-Wesley, 1954), vol. 1.

ment strivings.[3] As one learns, for example, about the pervasive influence of egoistic achievement needs in the technologically advanced nations, one begins to understand and appreciate the contrasts that appear in more affiliative societies.[4] One book explores both egoistic and altruistic behavior, laying out some of the antecedent conditions of both.[5] The important point is that there is nothing academic about this intellectual trek from early philosophy to contemporary social psychology. For those serious about making changes and improvements, it is a required reading (and thinking) assignment.

Social psychologists, then, consider it their scientific business to challenge simple and sovereign doctrines as well as more sophisticated ones, to construct fruitful ways of testing their validity, and to develop more comprehensive explanations of the social nature of man, explanations based on empirical facts. Because of the careful probing by social psychologists, simple and sovereign solutions have been clearly shown to be neither simple nor sovereign. When someone argues that all social behavior stems from man's egoism, he appears to be saying something fundamental. He seems to be able to explain a great deal with this assertion, not only instances of selfish disregard for others but also cases where people help one another because, the argument goes, they receive a selfish feeling of satisfaction or some other benefits from helping. But, we ask, how can one distinguish between egoistic helping and egoistic hurting? People usually do want to make just such distinctions. The assertion can still remain tenable if the theorist shifts ground and explains that "helping someone is different from hurting someone because helping occurs when selfishness has been temporarily satisfied," or that "there is less selfishness in helping than in hurting."

In either case the doctrine of human egoism is no longer simple. In the first, man's selfish nature has gained the property of being a *state* of satisfaction; in the second, a *quantity* of selfishness has been added When we reach this level of complexity, we are ready for some specific questions: Just how temporary is a "temporary satisfaction"? In what

[3] J. Macaulay and L. Berkowitz, eds., *Altruism and Helping Behavior* (New York: Academic Press, 1970); R. Christie and F. Geis, *Studies in Machiavellianism* (New York: Academic Press, 1970); D. C. McClelland, *The Achieving Society* (New York: Van Nostrand Reinhold, 1961).

[4] D. C. McClelland and D. G. Winter, *Motivating Economic Achievement* (New York: Free Press, 1969); G. Iacono, "An Affiliative Society Facing Innovations," *Journal of Social Issues* 24 (1968): 125–30; M. Cole, J. Gay, J. A. Glick, and D. W. Sharp, *The Cultural Context of Learning and Thinking* (New York: Basic Books, 1971).

[5] J. W. M. Whiting, B. Whiting, and R. Longabaugh, *Egoism and Altruism* (forthcoming).

circumstances does it occur? How much difference in "selfishness" is there between "helping" and "hurting"? And, most important of all, by what means are we to measure the differences in the amounts of these quantities? When these questions are answered, the original formulation then becomes testable and the really interesting work of social psychology can commence.

There is no general agreement among social psychologists on approaches to the study of man's social nature. In fact, they make quite different assumptions about social behavior, and their theoretical orientations to social-psychological problems differ as do their research strategies. We shall compare a few of the more important approaches now so that in subsequent chapters one can realize how much the types of research conducted and the conclusions drawn are determined by the theoretical assumptions made in the planning of experiments. The differences of approach are interesting in themselves and are useful because they lead to theoretical arguments that in turn stimulate further research.

One school of thought maintains that real progress will be made in understanding social behavior when social psychologists are content with describing the observable actions of people in various social contexts rather than theorizing about attitudes, feelings, or motives—that is, the nonobservable bases of behavior. Those who find this approach congenial play essential roles in the development of modern social psychology by producing reliable facts about behavior that later become the bases of sound theory. When we look into the rudimentary forms of social interaction and the acquaintance process in Chapter 5, or the effect of groups on individual behavior in Chapter 6, we shall demonstrate how necessary it is to describe each stage in the development of interpersonal associations and each aspect of the social contexts in which interaction takes place.

An opposing school of thought argues, however, that such an approach is too inductive, that it is primarily suited to the study of very simple forms of behavior but not appropriate for the explanation of complex social behavior. This school of thought believes that social psychologists should deal squarely with the complexities—the motives, attitudes, values, perceptual style of individuals, for example—and study how these personal dispositions develop, how they affect social behavior, and how they, in turn, are affected by social contacts. Although it seems straightforward enough, this approach is complex because it requires that the researcher concern himself with nonobservables. That is, he must create techniques for *inferring* the existence of attitudes or motives (neither of which can be directly observed) from careful observations of behavior in various social contexts. The task is much like that of the physicist who infers the existence of an atom from observing certain natural events that are presumed to depend on atomic activity. Neither attitudes nor atoms can be directly observed, but both can be indirectly measured. In fact, on the basis of such nonobservables, theories can be created that are as exciting and useful for social psychology as comparable ones are for the physical sciences. When we examine the development of motives and personality styles in Chapter 2 and the nature of social attitudes in Chapter 4, the potential value of this approach will become apparent.

There is one other important difference of viewpoint among contemporary social psychologists that will concern us. Some argue that too much attention in theory and research has been given to personality dispositions built up through long-term social experiences to the neglect of the more immediate influences that affect behavior. When a prisoner of war collaborates with his captors, the dissenter may ask, should we search for an explanation of his actions deep in his personality or in the immediate social setting pressuring him? Do people conform because they have particular dispositions built up over the years, or does *anyone* conform if the circumstances are made just right? Those who emphasize the short-term influences provide us with basic principles that tell us, for example, how to put pressure on someone to change his behavior. They also show us what the limits of such pressures are and what social and cultural contexts they work best in.

Many social psychologists now see value in both these approaches and design their research so that it can reflect the joint effects of short- and long-term influences. This recent movement encourages researchers to look painstakingly into both the learning process that shapes personal dispositions and the various aspects of the immediate social setting. We shall highlight this more comprehensive approach as much as possible. Jones and Nisbett, for example, have observed how we tend to attribute another person's behavior to his personal traits or disposition ("He's an aggressive person") whereas we attribute our own behavior to the eliciting situation ("I got angry because I was insulted").[6] Is it possible that even as social psychologists our theoretical biases rest on such habits of attribution? Do the traits that we, even as scientists, see in others exist more in our own minds than in the observed facts? Is *everyone*, in short, prone to project certain kinds of schematic orderings? If so, social psychologists must be very critical

---

[6] E. E. Jones and R. E. Nisbett, *The Actor and the Observor: Divergent Perceptions of the Causes of Behavior* (New York: General Learning Corp., 1971).

of their own bases for attribution, and must ferret out the rules or habits of attribution we all tend to use under specifiable conditions. Such attribution habits are themselves a revealing aspect of our human nature.

One of our purposes in this book is to communicate the conviction of social psychologists that, through careful study, man's social nature will be revealed and that as we begin to understand these complexities we also begin to understand ourselves. A second purpose is to communicate the fun and excitement enjoyed by social psychologists as their work progresses. Our chapters deal with some of the recurring social processes of contemporary interest. But since these are terribly complex matters, we must keep our knowledge about them in perspective. We have made only a beginning; in some cases hardly even that. But the pleasures, excitement, and hopes of the discipline can be clearly recognized in the beginnings themselves, even in the brief introduction to them we can present here.

In Chapter 2 we shall examine some of the ways that social influences leave their traces on individuals, especially young people who are being taught to be members of their societies. The focus of attention will be on the development of the child's conscience and his sense of identity, as well as the development of his dispositions toward aggressiveness, compliance, affiliation, and achievement. In other words, the emphasis will be placed on the broader categories of behavior that become integrated into distinctive personality styles. In .Chapter 3, the focus is shifted to the adjustments people make to their social environments—how they come to perceive and judge people and events in shared ways and in individualized ways. In Chapter 4 we look further into the ways people cope with their environments as we study how people's thoughts, feelings, and tendencies to react become organized around certain recurring social events. These organized modes of thinking, feeling, and reacting are referred to as *attitudes*, and we shall describe how they function, how they are measured, how they affect behavior, how they develop, and how they can be modified. In Chapter 5 our focus alternates between the individual and the events that take place between two or more people as they interact. We try to explain how associations among people become established, develop, or disintegrate, and how those involved are affected by the interaction. The same theme is elaborated further in Chapter 6 as we describe the psychological consequences of belonging to groups and try to explain why some people adjust their behavior to the social demands of groups and why others take advantage of the opportunities to become leaders. In that chapter we also discuss how variations in the organization of groups affect the action of members, how pride in groups develops and sometimes leads to intergroup conflict, and how personal conflict can arise when one tries to belong to potentially antagonistic groups. In the final chapter our view of groups is broadened to include societies and cultures, thus permitting us to look into the role that these more extensive groups play in shaping man's social behavior and permitting us to touch on the large question of the causal relationships that exist between the processes of social psychology and those of the other behavioral sciences.

:

Socialization

chapter two

Our personalities are shaped and developed in important ways through social contacts with other people. The process of socialization—learning to become a member of one's family, one's community, and one's national group—starts in infancy and progresses, with growth and learning, to the point where one behaves, thinks, feels, and evaluates in ways similar to everyone else in the society. An infant becomes a child whose behavior greatly resembles that of the other members of his family and social groups. Socialization is a lifelong process that continues at various rates in different circumstances. The process sometimes accelerates when, say, a liberally educated college graduate, capable of a broad range of thinking and evaluating, enters a large bureaucracy and gradually takes on the thoughts and judgments of his new community. What is the common theme among the various socialization experiences of different individuals? Current researchers and theorists are intent on determining what the elements of the socialization process are and how they interrelate to give that process its general form. Social psychology has many theories about the process. An oversimplified notion is that an individual becomes more and more like those around him. But this notion leads to the error of watching *only*

photo by Michael Semak

similarities. It may explain, for example, how a minister's son comes to resemble his quiet and serene father. although the boy has actually developed, through a hidden process of seething rebellion, all the qualities that make him a happy and successful Marine sergeant. Some of the most fascinating examples of socialization are the "failures": the daughters who rebel and act exactly as their mothers would not, the professional soldier who retires and becomes a pacifist, the well-brought-up generation that leads a revolution against society and tries to make fundamental changes in it.

Stephen Klineberg has highlighted with his research the explosive possibilities in the socialization of young people in the traditional area of the inner city of Tunis, Tunisia.[1] Parents hold to their ancient be-

[1] S. L. Klineberg, "Modernization and the Adolescent Experience: A Study in Tunisia," *The Key Reporter* 37, no. 1 (Autumn 1971): 2–4.

liefs and values emphasizing the absolute authority of the father (and the veil for the wife), with the father feeling pressure from Allah himself to pass on his heritage and faith to his children. Modern conditions have determined otherwise. Tunisia is spending a higher percentage of its income on education than any other country in the world. The result is that among schoolchildren, over 65 percent of the boys and 48 percent of the girls are so caught up with the modern values promulgated in school that they aspire to university training. Yet the system can only manage to give 15 percent of these young people a high school education and only 10 percent of these can go on to college. So the overall system is out of synchrony: the children do not tend to share the values of the parents, the system cannot satisfy the new hopes of the children for schooling, much less provide the huge number of professional-level jobs that students are now aiming for. Even the new generation has explosive differences within it, since 75 percent of the girls have dropped the traditional veil, and they are expecting a life of freedom and autonomy that the present crop of boys, even with their own new values, are not in the least prepared to accept.

Yet most societies reproduce their social values generation after generation, and the reasons why they can succeed in doing so are complex. Societies may perpetuate these similarities by conscious teaching or training of the young, or by imposing social pressures on all their members from birth to death, or by their failure to provide more satisfactory alternatives.

Another oversimplified notion is that certain people never really become socialized. Consider this example from Allison Davis and John Dollard.[2]

> At school, Julia's acquaintances (she has only one intimate friend and does not believe in forming a circle of close associates) call her "Raddie," meaning "rowdy," or "troublemaker," and she is regarded by both pupils and teachers as a "show-off." Julia herself boasts that the people at school, as well as the boy friends whom she curses and fights, think she is "crazy"; that is, that she will do "anything"—fight a man, curse a teacher, or kiss a boy in the schoolyard—without regard for the usual restrictions upon a girl and upon a pupil.... But Julia is a fighter and she does not bar even her mother. She replies that her mother does not like her and has never liked her.... A slender but tigerish Amazon who fights with her fists rather than with a knife, she harasses her boy friends with insatiable aggression until a curse and slap lead to a knockdown drag-out fight.

When we realize that this is a black girl from a lower-lower class

[2] A. Davis and J. Dollard, *Children of Bondage* (Washington, D.C.: Council on Education, 1940).

background in New Orleans, there should be no question about Julia being socialized: in fact, she may be very well trained and prepared for the seamy life she is likely to face.

Social psychologists have concentrated so far on the major social influences on personality development for two important reasons. First, knowing the conditions of personality development helps us focus on interpersonal or social processes and so improve our understanding of their relationship to adjustment, development, and learning. Second, personality development is itself an interpersonal process since inevitably it occurs through the influence of other people. Language and personal styles of speech, for example, can only be picked up from others, and language learning is a basic component of socialization as a whole.

Resocialization

To best illustrate the social psychology of personality formation, let us consider a famous instance of attempted personality destruction—the effort of the Chinese communists to desocialize American prisoners of the Korean War, to wipe out the effects of their previous socializtion. We base our discussion on the report of Edgar Schein, a social psychologist who interviewed many of the men on their release.[3] The Chinese attempted not only to wipe out the socialization of the American soldiers but also to resocialize them, to make the Americans believe in the political beliefs and values of Chinese communism. Although the Chinese did succeed in peripheral ways they failed in their basic aim. Their frail successes, however, give us insight into the juggernaut power of the usual massive socialization that all human beings continually pass through.

To desocialize a human to the point where he can be fundamentally changed requires a manipulation of the great social structures that control his sense of identity. The United States Army, like all military bodies, is set up to turn a man into a courageous soldier—a task requiring a powerful process of socialization. The Chinese first took officers away from their men, and with the officers went the constant rehearsal of learned roles that helps maintain army structure. Then the Chinese separated out the noncommissioned officers lest, through their role of leadership, they reinvigorate army structure and cohesion at the lower levels. They broke up companies and squads to leave each

---

[3] E. H. Schein, "The Chinese Indoctrination Program for Prisoners of War: A Study of Attempted 'Brainwashing,'" in *Readings in Social Psychology*, 3d ed., ed. E. E. Maccoby, T. M. Newcomb, and E. L. Hartley (New York: Holt, Rinehart & Winston, 1958), pp. 311–34.

man even more alone. They put minority-group members together so that lurking feelings of injustice might be exploited.

This policy of separation left only the less tangible structures of informal social organization—the friendships within the group and the minimal social structures required for day-to-day behavior. Even then, however, the captors were highly inventive in breaking friend from friend and preventing acquaintanceships from forming so that men might find peace with one another. Weak men were lured by special treatment into informing on their comrades and this special treatment became clear enough to the other prisoners to be demoralizing. Each prisoner, however, remained uncertain as to whether other men were also secret informers. Since knowing and liking another person requires trust, the principal aim of the Chinese was to destroy trust. Without it, the main social controls on everyday behavior would disappear.

Isolated and alone now, the men were then forced to listen to constant and clever propaganda devised to inculcate them with negative aspects of their former lives and the positive aspects of their future if they would take on the beliefs of their captors. But listening was not enough. The captives had to participate actively in their own retraining, but not all at once. They must first develop the habit of confessing trivial wrongdoings, such as minor infractions of prison rules. Such confession, reinforced by rewards, possibly would lead to a habit of public apology that might spread to other actions and deeper beliefs.

To become like persons in control may depend on the prisoners envying their power and privileges. And envy was easy for the Chinese captors to arrange. But they also had sense enough to know that they must themselves seem potentially likeable. Added to threats, then, were the lures that patience and kindness could provide, and the rewards that accrued from collaboration.

In summary, the men were made to feel alone, distrustful of each other, and afraid. Their minds were filled with constant propaganda, with proofs of the rewards of a change in their beliefs as well as proofs of the terror of resistance. To us in America, these brainwashing techniques were mysterious and frightening. Actually, however, we were seeing only a dramatic example of an ordinary technique, although this new perspective gave us insight into the factors that build up— or destroy—a human being's personal identity.

By and large, however, the Chinese failed, especially when they were dealing with mature men who were set against them. Some of the men did break, but usually because of some insufficiencies in their early socialization. Some men were bent, but straightened out when returned to their usual world. Others rebelled against the brainwashing and either died in prison or endured severe privations. Most of the men used their wits and just played along. Those who successfully survived gained a deepened insight into themselves and others. We do not know exactly why the Chinese failed, but their failure highlights the effectiveness and strength of the processes that had made these men into Americans and later into American soldiers. They had human ties and ideas that were hard to eradicate, personal bonds that mass methods could not loosen. They had traits, motives, and deep wishes that could only be expressed in their own culture. They were still able to fall back on their wit and intelligence and the healing balm of hearing their own language with all its familiar associations. The Chinese were not entirely attuned to all this, and their great effort could be partially frustrated by a Brooklyn-born soldier publicly reading a passage in Karl Marx with a humorous southern accent.

The Social Context of Personality Formation

Particular classes of social influences have an extensive impact on personality formation. Here we shall examine how community and family start their vigorous shaping process.

THE COMMUNITY

From infancy, a child learns the names and some of the properties of a number of people, and begins to pick up knowledge of the multiplicity of roles these people assume. With some individuals, and even with some groups, he may develop deep ties that influence the formation of his habits of judgment and action. These ties are critical both as a direct influence on later actions and as a source of models for behavior.

Roger G. Barker and Herbert F. Wright have studied the public side of these formative influences, summarizing them in terms of the number and kinds of *settings* in a child's life.[4] Their idea is that a growing child (or adult, for that matter) is formed in part by his many encounters with the hard-to-change qualities of the public settings of his community. People, they point out, are more manipulatable than the settings themselves. It is easier for a child who begins to ache from sitting on a church bench to move and wiggle than to change the seat, just as it is easier to go along with the traditional segregation of people expected in some settings than to change the setting itself.

[4] R. G. Barker and H. F. Wright, *Midwest and Its Children* (Evanston, Ill.: Row, Peterson, 1954).

Barker and Wright showed that it is possible to count all the public settings in a town and to treat each one as a scientific unit for social psychological study. Once all the settings are surveyed and described, they can be compared for similarity, so that the distinctive ones can be isolated. Some settings that were not sufficiently distinctive to be retained as separate settings for analysis—"the entrance to the drug store" and "the introductory speech at the local lodge"—were not kept as different from "the drug store" and "the lodge meetings," whereas it was useful to differentiate "the Baptist Church" and "the most popular local swimming place."

Barker selected all the reasonably distinct settings in an American town and in a larger but generally comparable English town.[5] The American town yielded 579 public settings for its 715 inhabitants; the English town had only 494 settings for its 1300 inhabitants; the ratios were 1.18 per person in "Midwest, U.S.A." and .55 per person in "Yoredale, England." These differences cast light on some of the sources of contrast between American and English character. In Midwest the average child fills 8.4 responsible positions in his community; in Yoredale only 2.7. Midwest adolescents play 16.6 responsible roles, Yoredale adolescents only 4.7. This difference continues into adulthood and old age. There are simply more settings in the American town, and the people are called on to fill roles in more settings. Children are also less segregated in the American town: 52 percent of all settings are open to them, whereas the English children are excluded from 77 percent of their town's settings.

Character is formed through such social contexts. Barker believes that the environment of behavior in America has been characterized not so much by an abundance of resources, but rather by a scarcity of people for the country's behavior settings.

Although the more resistant behavior settings may alter in time, the softer human actors change according to the immediate environment. According to Barker, each setting calls for an optimal number of participants; when there are too few participants, then those few will be more pressed, and pressed in more varied directions. In Midwest, rather than Yoredale, we might hear an adolescent told: "You may not know much about acting, but we have to find someone to play Hamlet!"

American children, then, participate more intensively in more settings than do their English cousins. Future research will investigate fully the results of intensive social participation. Can it be that because of

---

[5] R. G. Barker, "Ecology and Motivation," *The Nebraska Symposium on Motivation, 1960*, ed. M. R. Jones (Lincoln: University of Nebraska Press, 1960).

such greater pressure American character *is* what we sometimes think it is: active, resourceful, sociable, hopeful, and a bit anxious? Or does the existence of such a national character in the first place lead to the formation of such a great number of settings? Will American character change with an increase in population and with the continued movement from small towns to urban centers and back out to the suburbs?

Gump and Friesen have reported research focused on life in a large high school compared to a small one.[6] In small schools students report twice as many pressures from others to participate in the many activities of the school because such behavior settings are understaffed. In large schools only the more promising and gifted students find other people going out of their way to get them involved—about one third of the students report being left out altogether. It is interesting to speculate how many children feel when they move from a small high school to a large university and all the social requests they are used to suddenly disappear. The difficulty some college freshmen experience may stem from their attributing the loss (or sudden gain) of their social importance to their own personal failure, rather than to their having moved from an underpopulated setting to an overpopulated one (or vice-versa). We have, then, the beginning of a method for studying the potential influence of the qualities of settings on the malleable properties of the participants.

THE FAMILY

Of all formative influences on socialization, the family, which provides the nonpublic settings in a child's life, has received the most intensive study. Psychologists have turned a good deal of their attention to this area in recent years and are beginning to put important pieces together. Now we see in its full complexity the recurrent problem of social psychology—isolating facts for study—since, in addition to socialization, the internal psychological processes of both parent and child and the rapid, constant changes in the child as a result of physical maturation are factors to contend with, particularly in the family. In many studies these complications have received little or no attention. A new growth of interest in research on both animals and human beings has fostered the joint study of genetic factors and maturational stages *together with* social and other environmental influences.

In this discussion our focus is on differences among families and general social environments, and we will try to track down the principal

6 R. G. Barker and P. Gump, *Big School, Small School* (Stanford, Calif.: Stanford University Press, 1964), pp. 75–93, 94–135.

ways family pressures on a child differ from family to family and from society to society.

A study by researchers from Cornell, Harvard, and Yale isolated the important differences in families in small communities in six different cultures—Northern India, Okinawa, Mexico, Africa, the Philippines, and the northeastern United States.[7] A group of children was studied in each community and the youngsters' mothers were kind enough to give long interviews on how they and other family members dealt with the children, thereby providing much valuable information on the differences in pressures the children meet. This information was then reduced to seven major differences in family pressures listed below), and it turned out that these differences were due mainly to the ways individual mothers treated their children rather than from differences in culture.

Family settings differ greatly, then, in the following ways:

1. the demands for *responsibility* made on children, that is, the number and kinds of duties expected of them

2. the emotionally positive actions of mothers toward their children, such as praise, absence of physical punishment, and general *warmth*

3. the degree of control demanded over *aggression toward peers* both inside and outside the family

4. the degree of control over *aggression and disobedience toward parents*

5. the extent to which the mother does the *caretaking of babies*

6. the extent of her *caretaking of older children*

7. the degree of the mother's *emotional stability*, i.e., does she have an uneven temper?

Although an exhaustive list will only be possible when further research is carried out in many more cultures, this list does provide a tool for comparing private settings, and increases our realization of the immense and powerful differences we must consider when constructing theories of the processes of socialization and personality development. As we shall see below, some of these differences have already been uncovered in research into specific facets of socialization.

These differences in the family settings appear to arise from some very practical considerations. Families, who live surrounded by relatives, for example, are very strict about peer aggression, possibly because the related families are tied together in economic ways which might be disturbed if the younger members of the families fight with one another. In the United States, however, where there are large social

---

[7] B. Whiting, ed., *Six Cultures: Studies of Child Rearing* (New York: John Wiley, 1963); and W. W. Lambert and L. Triandis, "Pancultural Factor Analyses of Reported Socialization Practices," *Journal of Abnormal and Social Psychology* 62, no. 3 (May 1961): 631–39.

areas with no relatives' children in close proximity, it is possible for parents to be more permissive about peer aggression, with competent self-defense being more highly valued by the parents. Even maternal warmth, mentioned in item 2, may depend upon the size of the family—the greater the number of children, the less warmth—and the extent to which mothers do the caretaking of their children varies with such practical issues as to whether there are available adequate and low-cost replacements for themselves. William Lambert has suggested that most of the differences in family setting for a child arise from whether or not adequate *parental surrogates* are available, from the presence or absence of *target others* to practice helpfulness and aggression on, and whether or not the family or neighborhood contains *competitors* for the limited resources of parental energy, attention, and affection.[8]

John and Beatrice Whiting of Harvard have observed a fascinating relationship as part of the same six-culture study. Children who are trained to take on responsibility for herding large animals are the ones who appear to generalize these habits of responsibility in their behavior toward peers.[9] Responsible, adultlike behavior becomes part of the behavioral style of boys in East Africa and Northern India (the herding societies). This is a very different style from that of boys in the other four societies where the practical problems of large animal care are less important. In the New England case, for example, the goal of becoming a good student is important. This role calls for considerable delay of rewards and punishments, and calls forth individual achievement and observable arrogance rather than responsibility for maintaining group norms. In general, then, it appears that different conditions of socialization arise from the day-to-day pressures in family and community life.

Some Standards of the Socialization Process

Socialization starts when newborn children, complete with all their various (and largely unknown) genetic differences and their potential for rapid maturational changes, enter a world in which the various pressures from others begin to influence them in both public and private settings. Let us look at the developmental history of some of the

---

[8] W. W. Lambert and Rita Weisbrod, eds., *Comparative Perspectives on Social Psychology* (Boston: Little, Brown, 1971), pp. 54–56.

[9] B. B. Whiting and J. W. M. Whiting, "Task Assignment and Personality: A Consideration of the Effect of Herding on Boys," in *Comparative Perspectives on Social Psychology*, ed. W. W. Lambert and R. Weisbrod (Boston: Little, Brown, 1971).

strands of this process that psychologists have already described fairly adequately. Besides trying to unravel some of these threads, we shall begin to search for apparent common principles. Afterwards we shall attempt to see the process in its larger outlines.

SOCIAL COMPLIANCE

The Fels Institute at Antioch, Ohio, a leader in research on socialization, has focused on the conditions under which children come to comply with the commands and suggestions of other people.[10] Their strategy calls for an examination of the home pressures on the control of aggression and disobedience, the fourth factor uncovered in the six-culture study mentioned above. In the Fels Institute study children of different ages are observed at home and at school so that their compliance tendencies can be placed in the context of their total behavior.

The Fels researchers discovered that compliance tendencies begin rather diffusely but become more consistent as the child matures. Thus, it is not possible to predict whether a three- to five-year-old child will be compliant or resistant at school from a knowledge of his parents' policies of reward and punishment. But it is possible to make predictions on the basis of this knowledge for older children, and (as is often found with other strands of socialization) rewards appear to be more effective than punishments in inducing compliance.

As children become older, their compliant behavior becomes increasingly consistent. Nursery-school children are somewhat uniform in complying with adults both at home and at school, but are not so with peers. Consistency in compliance with both peers and adults is more pronounced with older (six-, seven-, and eight-year-old) children.

In its relation to children's overall behavior, compliance shifts toward a more central position from the early to later years. A nursery-school child who is compliant with his peers tends also to be generally dependent on them for physical help, emotional support, and approval. At the same time, however, he tends to be aggressive or hostile towards them. In contrast, the young child who is compliant with adults, and is ready to do things on his own, is marked by low aggressiveness and dominance. In short, when a child is young, dependency is related to compliance with peers but it is not related to compliance with adults.

Adjustment to adults is basic to the older child's general adjustment. At six to eight years, help-seeking and dependency no longer distinguish the children who are compliant with peers, and those who are compli-

[10] V. J. Crandall; S. Orleans; A. Preston; and A. Rabson, "The Development of Social Compliance in Young Children," *Child Development* 29 (June 1958): 429–44.

ant with adults are no longer markedly self-reliant. What is left is a consistent difference in dominance and aggressiveness, the compliant children exhibiting less of each quality than the noncompliant youngsters exhibit. Each child now behaves much more the same way toward peers as toward adults, at home and at school. Public and private pressures and his own maturation have resulted in a clear and consistent pattern by the time a child is eight. He has now become either a dominant or a submissive person. But these traits no longer seem to have anything to do with sociability or independence. Socialization and maturation have led to more consistent behavior with regard to compliance, but compliance no longer seems related to other traits as before.

As one facet of socialization, social compliance apparently involves a long sequence of learning. Children form habits of compliance as a consequence of the kinds of rewards and punishments the parents use or the models of behavior they present. These habits of compliant behavior are generalized early to other adults who supervise them in nursery school, and eventually come to characterize their behavior with peers. We might say that compliant behavior is a special case of *instrumental learning* (the process whereby habits are shaped by the temporal relation of their occurence with respect to rewards and punishments) and that this process is managed by various other important people, especially parents.

In this example we have not discovered whether these American children are more or less compliant (or dominating and aggressive) than children from other cultures—that would require a more complex research plan. Nor have we ruled out the possibility that compliance or dominance may be due to gene structure. Heredity may determine the direction of a child's development, or it may cause a child to behave so that his parents may—for their own comfort or because of their sensitivity to social norms—attempt to manipulate his development through rewards or punishments. To discount this possibility would require more knowledge of genetics than we now have.

Nor have we ruled out other explanations. Those familiar with Freudian terminology may suggest that the growth of such behavioral consistency from nursery school to grade school occurred as the child *internalized* parent values in coming to identify with the opposite-sex parent (thus resolving the Oedipus or Electra complex). Others would point to the greater consistency of parental pressures toward older children, claiming that their more consistent behavior merely reflected this concerted pressure at home, as well as the increasing pressure in the older children's public settings toward playing roles calling for consistent dominance (being a leader) or consistent compliance (being a follower). Thus, as children grew older their behavior would shift and differentiate in response to the direction of these immediate pressures. Plainly, available interpretations of the socialization process are numerous and rich.

Despite the technical and theoretical issues raised, the study we have been discussing points up some clear relationships that help us see the developmental history of compliance among some American children. A start has been made here, and the variety of possible interpretations with regard both to the facts and their theories of compliance need not confuse us; they will lead to further studies that will eliminate unfruitful alternatives. It is the fruitfulness of the research derived from a theory that is consequential, not the brilliance of the argument presented.

AGGRESSIVENESS

We have already mentioned that the more compliant youngster is relatively less aggressive. This may be of only incidental interest in the study of compliance, but since all cultures attempt to control aggressiveness, it often takes the center of the stage. The development of aggressiveness seems to have a more complicated history than does compliance; but this may be so merely because we know more about it. Most psychological matters turn out to be complex once we begin to study them.

A good deal of interest in aggression was stimulated by Leonard Doob and his colleagues.[11] They developed a specific principle of behavior relating frustration and aggression. Some form of frustration precedes aggressive behavior, but frustrations do not always lead to aggression (though they *tend* to) since other behavior (such as compliance) may conflict or interfere with its expression. Research on the implications of this principle has shown its usefulness. But the frustration-aggression hypothesis does not deal directly with a number of instances of aggressiveness. For one, some people when frustrated express aggression more readily than do others: Is this merely the result of past frustrations (including punishments)), or have rewards for being aggressive played a part? For another, some people are aggressive with no apparent instigation: Is this a different form of aggressive behavior (sadism, say, as opposed to retaliation)? Are there still other forms of aggressiveness that people learn to use—socially acceptable aggression rather than antisocial aggression, playful aggression rather than serious attack, and so on?

Aggression has many outlets. Often it is displaced, as when the child kicks the dog because he is not allowed to kick his parents. Aggression is attenuated, as when we retaliate an attack by sarcasm or

---

[11] L. Doob et al, *Frustration and Aggression* (New Haven, Conn.: Yale University Press, 1939).

merely by entertaining an aggressive wish. Aggression is projected, as when an aggressive man only sees other people as aggressive, never himself; or when he calls others aggressive in order to justify an aggressive act he has committed. A great deal of work remains to be done in specifying how aggression is instigated: Is aggression-in-anger less effective in eliciting counteraggression than aggression-in-cold-reason? Is injustice as vital as a physical blow in arousing aggression? Does the intention of the other person play an important part in arousing aggression? If so, what are the social conditions under which "malevolent intention" is inferred? What is the influence of mutual trust or distrust on the interpretation of an aggressive act? As for the *reduction* of aggression, there are also many questions to be answered. Suppose B hits A but A is not permitted to hit back: does this increase A's aggressive tendency? Suppose A does hit back: does this decrease his aggressiveness or merely make him feel guilty? Suppose B hits A but C (for another reason) hits B: does the sight or knowledge of this event reduce or enhance A's urge to retaliate? One of the great practical issues involved in all these questions is what effects do aggressive models have on a television audience (or on readers or theatergoers, etc.).

Questions of this sort have stimulated various studies of aggression

Some effects of violence on audience

in recent years. For example, how does a growing child pick up and incorporate in his own repertoire the aggressive tendencies and behavior of those around him? Some fascinating answers have been uncovered for some American children by Robert Sears aid his colleagues.[12] Sears discovered that overly aggressive children are likely to come from homes where rules about aggressiveness are permissive but where punishment for acting aggressive is heavy. Conversely, the least aggressive children have been confronted with strong rules against aggression (which work to prevent it) but with nonpunitive means of dealing with it. Permissive rules apparently contribute more to making a child aggressive than heavy punishment does. Sears's information came from reports by the mothers themselves and must be applied only tentatively as yet to wider ranges of data.

Sears then followed up a large number of these same young children and again measured their aggressiveness when they were adolescents.[13] His questionnaire took into consideration many forms of aggressiveness possible by the age of twelve: antisocial aggression, attenuated aggression, self-aggression, and projected aggression. According to this follow-up study, where parents maintain the same pressures on the children, high permissiveness still results in high antisocial aggressiveness at age twelve; however, the heavily punished children now tend to be among the least antisocially aggressive.

This apparent shift between ages six and twelve in the effect of punishment lends support to an important and useful theory that has recently developed. The dilemma children face by having aggressive tendencies while simultaneously fearing the consequences of acting on them produces a state called *conflict drive*. Where the conflict is great, because of a long history of being punished, a strong, or explosive, tendency toward aggressiveness will be evident at age six. But since by age twelve children who have been heavily punished tend to be among the least aggressive ones, continued punishment has presumably reduced conflict by leading the children, in effect, to give up antisocial aggression because of the very heavy inhibition now associated with it.

This principle of a drive, or tension, produced by conflict has been independently applied in many contexts. Fritz Heider found conflict drive operating in the realm of ideas;[14] Leon Festinger used conflict

---

[12] R. R. Sears, E. E. Maccoby, and H. Levin, *Patterns of Child Rearing* (Evanston, Ill.: Row, Peterson, 1957).

[13] R. R. Sears, "Relation of Early Socialization Experiences to Aggression in Middle Childhood," *Journal of Abnormal and Social Psychology* 63 (November 1961): 466–95.

[14] F. Heider, *The Psychology of Interpersonal Relations* (New York: John Wiley, 1958).

drive, as we will see later, to analyze the effects of *dissonance* follow-ing a decision;[15] and Charles Osgood used conflict drive in the study of *incongruity* created by different pressures for attitude change.[16] Other versions and implications of the same principle are found in the works of other psychologists. In short, conflict drive in its various con-texts and formulations is of general relevance to all phases of the study of socialization. Indeed, one basic theoretical problem now facing so-cial psychologists is to determine which is the more powerful influence in human behavior—the reduction of conflict drive (in search of in-ward consistency), or the effects of direct rewards or punishments.

Attenuated aggression is different from antisocial aggression. Among the twelve-year-olds attenuated aggression tends to occur among highly punished children who have also lived under permissive aggression rules. This more acceptable aggression emerges by age twelve when aggressive behavior has been inhibited earlier through successful punish-ment techniques, so that it can be let out only in diluted form. Often attenuated aggression is accompanied by anxiety over being aggressive and some tendency toward self-aggression.

Sears also reported sex differences in aggressive tendencies. Ameri-can boys resort more to antisocial aggression while girls resort to at-tenuated aggression. American girls, in general, are less overtly aggres-sive than boys are; girls also have more anxiety over being aggressive. These differences may be genetic or they may reflect the different ways of raising boys and girls in America.

Clearly then, aggression is not a single, simple phenomenon. Sears's work, however, provides us with some psychological insights into ag-gression. We also gain some ideas about how certain components of aggression show up in the behavior of the growing child.

The study of six cultures, mentioned earlier, has also revealed some interesting facts about the development of *overt* aggressive actions.[17] If we lump together verbal aggression, hitting, and playful hitting, we find that although girls are less aggressive in all six cultures, there is, interest-ingly, no general decrease in rates of observed aggression with age (up to ten years). This is possibly because most of the punishment (and en-couragement) for aggression outside the home is given by other chil-dren—often younger children—and we could hardly expect that they would shape this behavior very effectively. We should quickly add, how-ever, that although aggression as a *whole* does not decrease with age,

---

15 L. Festinger, *A Theory of Cognitive Dissonance* (Evanston, Ill.: Row, Peterson, 1957).

16 C. Osgood et al., *The Measurement of Meaning* (Urbana: University of Illinois Press, 1957).

17 W. W. Lambert, in preparation.

there are changes in some of the components and in the situations where it occurs as children get older. First, plain hitting *does* decrease with age, generally. Further, older children learn to decrease their aggression when adults are around. They learn to ease off on their bickering when close to home, to let off steam toward nonfamily members rather than siblings, and to do this while playing rather than in social, school, or work situations. Another intriguing and still mysterious (and not yet published) fact has emerged: There is a general tendency for boys to immediately retaliate when they are being "picked on" (or ignored, hit, insulted, hit playfully) about one-third of the time, while girls do so about one-fourth of the time. The mystery enters when we note that this retaliation tendency does not vary with the ages or the cultures which have been studied to date, although considerable individual differences exist.

At this stage, of course, the work of Sears and of the six-culture study is limited in the number of children studied, the measures used, the weakness of the relationships discovered, and geographical range. But both studies provide suggestive facts and examples of current theories. There are, as usual, alternative interpretations of the facts. It may be, for instance, that aggressive children in Sears's study are merely aping their punitive parents at age six, and that by twelve they drop antisocial for socially acceptable aggression because they have learned that the punishments by their parents are socially acceptable whereas their own past forms of aggression have not been. Or they may act aggressively in a permissive household on the rational supposition that they can get away with it. Or again, the findings may reflect changes in the public settings or changes in parental or peer pressures as the child grows older. It may also reflect the effects of that mysterious phenomenon of identification that we mentioned in connection with the socialization of compliance. What do we know about this phenomenon?

IMITATION

It was once fashionable to think of imitation as the simple, sovereign, and universal social psychological process that could explain most social behavior of men and animals. Imitation, it was said, is part of human nature, an instinctive tendency to do what others do. But such a simple assumption hides complexity, as simple doctrines often do. Some people imitate more than others do, children imitate more than adults do, and people often do the opposite of what others do. Neal Miller and John Dollard thought of imitation as a form of social learning. They demonstrated experimentally that it is possible for white rats (as well as children) to learn a habit of imitating if they are adequately rewarded.[18] As rewards increased, so did the tendency to follow a leader. In time a generalized habit of following developed that carried over to other situations and to other leaders. With children, the leader could easily teach the follower how to copy, and though the process may lead the second person to behave the same way as the first, it is not simple imitation. The same behavior might also occur because both follower and leader have learned in the past to respond similarly to the same cues; but again, this imitation is not necessarily simple and instinctive. The relevant case, then, is called *matched-dependent behavior,* the situation where a more experienced leader's behavior is the cue to a less experienced follower. What are the conditions, if any, under which the follower will stop waiting for the actions of the leader and perform on his own?

Russell Church has provided at least one answer to this question.[19] Working with rats, he found that even these little creatures can pick up *incidental cues* that lead to successful outcomes, although they are not necessarily those the leader uses. Incidental cues are naturally present when a correct response is made but absent (or different) for an incorrect response. By way of illustration, suppose a child is following his mother walking on the stones in a creek bed. The mother avoids stones that are likely to be slippery because they have been covered by water. The child, however, learns to use gray stones but to avoid green ones (which are also wet). Thus, in a similar situation, he may behave correctly, even when his model is not there, by using the cue "greenness" in place of his mother's cue of "slipperiness." The child may have learned to do so whether or not he can say *what* he learned; he has settled on these cues because they have been reliably successful. Through such subtle incidental cues culture may sometimes be transmitted from older to younger members—through manners, skills, games, language habits, and styles. Such differences in perceiving cues may underlie the arguments that arise between generations.

VICARIOUS SOCIALIZATION

Children acquire habits of imitation, then, some habits more rapidly than others. Although we have no proofs as yet, it is likely that first-born children, who have more extensive contact with expert, patient, and verbally active adult models, learn to imitate more thoroughly than do later-born children, whose models are often their inept and impatient

---

[18] N. E. Miller and J. Dollard, *Social Learning and Imitation* (New Haven, Conn.: Yale University Press, 1941).

[19] R. Church, "Two Procedures for the Establishment of 'Imitative Behavior,'" *Journal of Comparative and Physiological Psychology* 50 (June 1957): 315–19.

older siblings. Children also develop habits of *applying* incidental cues (such as our example of "greenness") learned from situations in which they have had models to follow to other situations where models are not available. They do so, of course, with varying degrees of success in the new situations.

These habits of imitation are way stations to the still richer possibilities of vicarious learning through observation. When one child in a family or in school watches another child being taught, he learns a good deal by just watching. Seymour Berger has experimentally demonstrated that under certain conditions the watcher's learning may equal or even exceed that of the pupil, even though the watcher received no observable feedback for success or failure.[20] The watcher, perhaps, in imitating the pupil responds *covertly* or internally (along with the person being taught, who is responding *overtly*), and is affected by his own covert successes and failures. Later, when the model is no longer there, the watcher is able to act overtly according to his covertly learned responses.

The importance for children of observational learning is now being carefully examined. Perceptive psychologists at the turn of the century emphasized the child's learning through observation. For example, James M. Baldwin argued that a child goes through stages of passively taking in the activities of those about him and only later starts to imitate the actions and the attitudes of others.[21] But this line of thinking was largely bypassed until recently when Jerome Bruner, studying in Africa, was struck by how extensively children learn through observation:

> What the child knows, he learns from direct interaction with the adults' community . . . in thousands of feet of film, one sees no *explicit* teaching in the sense of a "session" out of the context of action to teach the child a particular thing. It is all implicit.[22]

The recent work of Michael Cole and his colleagues also emphasized that "children learn more from observation than from situations specially designed to transmit information orally."[23]

We have, of course, a great deal to learn about the conditions under which a watcher will vicariously practice the role of another. Some particularly favorable conditions may be when the model is doing something the watcher values, when the model is a friend rather than an enemy, and when both the model's cues and responses are clear. When

[20] S. Berger, "Incidental Learning Through Vicarious Reinforcement," *Psychological Reports* 9 (1961): 477–91.

[21] J. M. Baldwin, *Social and Ethical Interpretations in Mental Development* (New York: Macmillan, 1897).

[22] J. S. Bruner, R. Oliver, and P. Greenfield, *Studies in Cognitive Growth* (New York: John Wiley, 1966).

[23] M. Cole et al., *The Cultural Context of Learning and Thinking* (New York: Basic Books, 1971), p. 39.

such possibilities have been studied we shall have revealed two important social psychological processes: *imitation* and *vicarious learning*. Probably the most ambitious research in this area is that of Albert Bandura of Stanford and his colleagues, who have experimentally studied the conditions under which children will model their behavior according to the example of the behavior of others.[24]

IDENTIFICATION

Identification is closely related to these two processes of imitation and vicarious socialization. Often, in fact, these three strands are not differentiated, and as yet no standard terminology exists for doing so. The notion of identification has grown, in part, out of Freudian theory; some researchers even feel that the term should be applied only to clinically bizarre and apparently unconscious phenomena wherein a patient may have guilt feelings toward his parents.

However, let us consider identification as a process separate from psychopathology. When a child behaves as if he feels like, acts like, and thinks like a particular other person, we can observe the process of identification. Along with Church's notion of incidental cues, this idea of identification explains how, for example, a child learns to be like a parent without receiving any apparent reward for so doing. Although this learning may take place simply because the child has decided covertly to practice the behavior of an important other person, the intensity and results of identification are so great that to many researchers it is the most crucial issue in all of social psychology. We shall look at the results of some studies based on identification.

John W. M. Whiting has developed a theory based on envy.[25] Because a child—and everyone, for that matter—wants to be like the person he envies, he begins to practice covertly the roles of those he envies. In fantasies and daydreams a person includes those (parents or others) who normally provide for his wants and establish his values, although these individuals are not necessarily the focus of the envy. In fantasies, these individuals appear in their usual roles of providers, and not as persons the child would like to be or replace. More likely, the parent who has proven his power to *withhold* the resources the child has learned to value—food, money, affection, freedom from fear or pain, and so on—will become the object of vicarious practice and therefore of covert learning. The indulgent parent is often surprised

24 A. Bandura, *Social Learning Theory* (New York: General Learning Corp., 1971).
25 J. W. M. Whiting, "Resource Mediation and Learning by Identification," in *Personality Development in Children*, ed. I. Iscoe and M. Stevenson (Austin: University of Texas Press, 1960).

when his child begins to behave like a restrictive parent or, temporarily, like an unpleasant or fearful television character. Another example of an envy-eliciting model is that of the business leader who maintains loyalty and efficiency in his subordinates by keeping a personal distance from them, thus increasing the value of his personal attention.

The Whitings also feel that the herding boys (mentioned earlier as part of the six-culture study) are doing a task that is considered very important by their parents. Consequently, the parents severely punish negligence, and the parental task-assigner looms very powerfully as a resource controller. The herd boys, therefore, envy the status of the assigner and covertly practice his role, thereby internalizing not only some responsible habits but an authoritative personal style that shows up strongly in their behavior towards those peer targets who are available for such role practicing.

Of course, there is a great gap between covertly practicing the role of the person identified with and overtly playing it. For many boys in America, the early years are dominated by their mothers rather than

Peer enforcement of role values

by their fathers. Although these boys may covertly practice their mothers' roles, they would be shamed or punished for overtly behaving in a feminine manner. Thus, although such observational learning may remain part of the growing boy's self-image, being feminine may never emerge as overt role-playing. It often shows up in more subtle ways.

At Harvard's Laboratory of Human Development, for instance, Lyn Carlsmith started with the knowledge that college men usually score higher on quantitative aptitude tests than on verbal aptitude tests, whereas college women score higher on verbal than quantitative tests. The score patterns for college freshmen whose fathers had been away during World War II were compared with those whose fathers had remained at home. The verbal and quantitative scores for the first group showed far smaller differences than the scores for the latter group. That is, the test scores for those boys whose fathers were away from home during the war showed a less masculine pattern. A replication of the study revealed that the difference between the verbal and quantitative scores was directly related to the length of the father's absence—the smaller the difference in scores, the longer the absence. Although these boys with absent fathers may well have taken on the overt masculine roles, they still showed the influence of the covert female roles picked up when their mothers were the most powerful people around. Irvin Child has recently emphasized a recurring pattern found in cross-cultural work: The boy who has identified with his mother often will be prone to violent, delinquent, male-chauvinist behavior at a later age, possibly as an overreaction in the struggle to become acceptably masculine.[26] Early absence of the father sets up conditions for mother-identification, with the young boy showing early effeminate behavior and low aggressiveness. In adolescence, however, the boy shows exaggerated aggressive behavior, and maintains a latent femininity. Cultures where no father figure is at hand for the young boys tend to have higher rates of crime.

These findings highlight the pervasive influence of imitation, vicarious social learning, and identification. Although these processes influence a child throughout his life, they are particularly strong in the early years of socialization when one or two people appear to a child to have potent control over his needs and values. In no other stage of life, except in extreme circumstances, does so much depend upon so few; if such a situation should arise again, then conditions might be appropriate for basic personality changes.

In another study of identification,[27] Lionel M. Lazowick compared

26 E. Zigler and I. Child, "Socialization," in *Handbook of Social Psychology*, vol. 3, ed. G. Lindzey and E. Aronson (Reading, Mass.: Addison-Wesley, 1969), p. 531. See Lyn Carlsmith, "Effect of Early Father Absence on Scholastic Aptitude," *Harvard Educational Review* 1, no. 34 (Winter 1964): 3–21.

27 L. M. Lazowick, "On the Nature of Identification," *Journal of Abnormal and Social Psychology* 51 (June 1955): 175–83.

quantitatively the similarity between parents and their college-age children in·how they evaluated a number of concepts. He held that this similarity of values is a measure of the strength of the subtle, sometimes still covert, identifications that exist among members of a family. Lazowick found that similarities in concept evaluations were greater between fathers and sons than between fathers and daughters, whereas mothers and daughters were no more alike than mothers and sons. When Lazowick then related these similarities to the general anxiety of the sons and daughters, it turned out that the less anxious boys are closer in their evaluation of concepts to both their mothers and fathers than are highly anxious boys. The trend is similar, although not statistically reliable, for girls. Lazowick's findings measure the influence of mothers (as well as fathers) in the socialization of American boys and also suggest that cross-sex identification is not necessarily harmful to the boys concerned.

An interesting new research procedure permits us to examine more carefully both cross-sex identification and parent-to-parent variations in socialization techniques. Mary Rothbart and Eleanor Maccoby developed tape recordings of a four-year-old child demanding attention of a parent ("Mama, come help me with my puzzle!") asking for help, pestering, becoming insolent ("This is a stupid puzzle, and . . ."), asking for unreasonable privileges, or being aggressive with a peer or a younger sibling.[28] The child's talk and the spontaneous reactions of the parents on the tape recordings was all too familiar and real for comfort when parents listened to the tapes. Rothbart and Maccoby's study showed that mothers were much more permissive toward sons than daughters; boys, for example, were permitted to be more aggressive toward mothers and more comfort-seeking. Similarly, American fathers were more permissive toward daughters than toward sons. This tape-recording technique of study has recently been extended and applied to different social groups by researchers at McGill University.[29] In Canada, they found, there was much less cross-sex permissiveness. However, according to the study's samples of Canadian working-class parents there was an important cultural difference: English-Canadian mothers were much more dominant in the socialization process than were English-Canadian fathers, while French-Canadian fathers were dominant in French-Canadian families. The relevance of mother-dominance compared with father-dominance for the development of achievement

[28] M. Rothbart and E. Maccoby, "Parents' Differential Reactions to Sons and Daughters," *Journal of Personality and Social Psychology* 4 (September 1966): 237–43.

[29] W. E. Lambert, A. Yackley, and R. N. Hein, "Child Training Values of English Canadian and French Canadian Parents," *Canadian Journal of Behavioral Science* 3 (June 1971): 217–36.

drive in children will be discussed later in this chapter and then we can better appreciate the influence of socialization values on personality development.

CONSCIENCE

Educators, parents, and people in general are all concerned with the development of *conscience*. Winfred Hill revealed that "good behavior"—our index of a person's strength of conscience—could well be learned simply through reward and punishment, through conditioning or learning to avoid some acts, or through various forms of vicarious learning.[30] This is particularly true for learning to resist temptation even when parents or teachers are absent, and for developing habits of obeying the rules for good behavior.

What is difficult to explain about conscience is why people feel guilty when they have done what they believe they ought not to have done. Hill points out that feeling guilty often involves self-criticism, a search for authorities who will accept a confession and apply punishments that supply relief, or a seeking out of some other form of punishment. We behave as if we wish to hurt ourselves—or arrange to get ourselves hurt by others—in retribution for having broken a rule. In this way we can reduce the tensions from feelings aroused by the difference between what we have done and what we ought to have done. Confession, as a matter of fact, may be so satisfying to some people that it comes to reinforce their habits of sinning.

An instructive empirical study by Robert Sears and his colleagues showed that children with strong consciences are likely to have been brought up with love-oriented techniques (such as praise, isolation, and the withdrawal of love) instead of material-oriented methods (material rewards or the withdrawal of privileges) or physical punishment. Hill, however, suggests that the development of conscience depends on the kind of learning that is rewarded when the love-oriented discipline is imposed. He suggests that a child who has done something wrong is put under parental disapproval until he has performed some *symbolic renunciation* of his wrongdoing, such as making an apology, making restitution, promising not to do the misdeed again or taking personal blame. Then the relaxation of the parental tension serves as the child's reward for the renunciation. When the child is physically punished or when privileges or material objects are withheld from him, no such renunciation is required and the issue is resolved more quickly. Although

[30] W. F. Hill, "Learning Theory and the Acquisition of Values," *Psychological Review* 67 (September 1960): 317–31.

external punishment is sometimes more comfortable for the child, it does less to strengthen his habits of renouncing and confessing.

Hill's findings imply that parents may produce a strong conscience in a child with any form of discipline so long as symbolic renunciation is reinforced and maintained as an automatic habit that eventually will apply *before* a wrong act is committed. This habit of feeling conscience-stricken is no simple thing to achieve and we often develop too much conscience, as Freud suggested, or too little, as others have argued.

Despite these difficulties of too much or too little, we are now on the threshold of important new advances in this age-old questioning of the nature of conscience. For instance, recently James Bryan and Perry London have found that children are more likely to develop an altruistic concern for others if family members encourage the child's expression of feelings and if the parents provide examples of cooperativeness rather than competitiveness and status-seeking.[31]

Some lasting effects of conscience development have been highlighted by Norma Haan and others.[32] Their approach was to study the habits of moral reasoning of college students and Peace Corps volunteers. Using the Kohlberg Moral Judgment Scale, Haan divided the students into two groups: those who used "principled moral reasoning" (morality according to shareable standards) and those who used "conventional moral reasoning" (morality according to conventional expectations). Students in the first group were politically and socially more activist in college and they were more liberal than their liberal parents than were the students in the second group. The principled moral reasoners also displayed more conflict and sense of separation from their families than did the conventional moral reasoners. Perhaps such conflict is one of the costs of moral maturity, although our knowledge in this area is still very limited.

STAGE FRIGHT

Social psychologists pay particular attention to those strands of the socialization process that are most relevant to later social behavior. Although conscience, identification, and imitation have lasting consequences, how a person develops sensitivity to audiences—whether he avoids them or seeks them out with delight—is also important.

Allan Paivio has started to look carefully into the antecedents of audi-

[31] J. H. Bryan and P. London, "Altruistic Behavior by Children," *Psychological Bulletin* 73 (March 1970): 200–211.

[32] N. Haan, M. Brewster Smith, and J. Block, "Moral Reasoning of Young Adults," *Journal of Personality and Social Psychology* 10 (May 1968): 183–201.

ence sensitivity.[33] Paivio measured stage fright in children by way of a specially designed questionnaire and then related this measure to information about the children's upbringing obtained from their parents. When parents rewarded their children frequently, punished them infrequently, and encouraged them in their social behavior, the youngsters developed little stage fright or embarrassment in publicly expressing themselves. More pronounced degrees of stage fright were associated both with unfavorable parental evaluations of the children's social behavior and with frequent punishments for failure to meet parental standards. Imitation and identification also seem to operate in developing stage fright, since the children of outgoing parents tend to be relatively unafraid of audiences. The development of exhibitionist searching for audiences, apparently not the same thing as merely being unafraid, is not clear to us as yet; but we do know that it is related to positive parental evaluation of a child's social comportment.

Alfred Baldwin and his colleagues found that exhibitionism and self-consciousness both predict how long a child will talk in front of an audience.[34] Children who are low on exhibitionism or high on self-consciousness tend to shorten their public speaking times more than children who are exhibitionist or unself-conscious. On the other hand, children who are both attracted to and fearful of the audience make the most speech errors. These same measures predict the willingness of a child to participate in a public performance on skit night at camp.

Stage fright and exhibitionism are good examples of two problems that fascinate social psychologists: how people develop particular traits as a result of social interaction, and also how these traits interrelate to produce later more complicated behavior.

AFFILIATION

Recently, Stanley Schachter reopened an issue in the study of socialization that earlier researchers had found rather fruitless—that of birth order.[35] In a study of some college students he discovered (to his own surprise) that a person's position in the birth order of his family is related to his choice of remaining alone or being with others when faced with a frightening situation. A majority of firstborn or only children

[33] A. Paivio et al., "Measures and Correlates of Audience Anxiety ('Stage Fright')," *Journal of Personality* 27 (March 1959): 1–17.

[34] H. Levin et al., "Audience Stress, Personality, and Speech," *Journal of Abnormal and Social Psychology* 61 (September 1960): 469–73.

[35] S. Schachter, *The Psychology of Affiliation* (Stanford, Calif.: Stanford University Press, 1959).

reported that they chose to be with others in a frightening situation, whereas most of those who were later-born chose to face their worry alone. Of course, the degree of fright may be important in this relationship, and firstborn or only children tend to have (or at least to report) greater fear. Even with highly anxious people, the same results related to order of birth are found. Schachter found that this effect shows up most clearly in an anxiety-producing or threatening situation. It is not related to family size, but rather to absolute order of birth. A fourth-born person, for instance, is even more likely to want to be alone than is a second-born person. These findings are of interest in that they were determined only after many other researchers had dismissed birth order as a rather insignificant factor in socialization.

Schachter was a good social psychological detective here. He looked back into the early period of personality formation to discover what there is about being firstborn that might explain why some people prefer being alone or with company in frightening situations. After reviewing past literature, Schachter's best hunch was that dependency is highly developed in the first child by oversolicitous and inexperienced parents. The firstborn is given more care than later children receive and is more often breast-fed. Ratings of boys and girls in a nursery school showed that firstborns tend to seek help, proximity, physical contact, attention, and recognition from adults more than do later-born children. Firstborn children draw on these dependency habits especially when they feel anxious. This is only a tentative interpretation, and further research is needed.

Schachter looked to later behavior where a difference in dependency might show up. He found indications that firstborns are more likely to seek psychotherapy, while later-borns prefer to solve their own problems.

Additional differences were detected. More later-borns became alcoholics than would be expected from their percentage in the population; fewer fighter pilots who were firstborn children become aces (with five or more kills), perhaps because of their higher anxiety. Harold H. Kelley has provided further evidence suggesting that firstborns may handle power struggles differently than do later-borns.[36] Firstborns try to get their own way through means that will not alienate others, whereas later-borns are more willful, regardless of the consequences. The firstborn seems to like to leave his adversaries feeling subordinated, a preference that may stem from power strategies learned in the home. The firstborn, as we have seen, is dependent and anxious and learns first to deal with unbeatable adults; the later-born, less dependent and

[36] H. H. Kelley, *Report to NSF*, Grant NSF-G553, 1961.

less scared, learn early to deal with a firstborn who can be frightened by a straight power-play. Schachter's findings, like all good scientific findings, cast light on old questions and gives us the opportunity to illuminate new ones.

Schachter has two suggestions regarding the value to a firstborn in facing trouble with others rather than alone. First, the presence of others directly reduces his anxiety; second, he can satisfy his desire for self-evaluation by watching others and comparing his own reactions in the situation with theirs. "Know thyself" may be an admonition created by a firstborn child.

Walter Toman of West Germany has recently elaborated some of the more global possibilities of the relationship between birth order and later personal affiliation.[37] His hypothesis is that if we marry (or befriend) someone who *duplicates* our childhood social conditions then our marriage or our friendship will be more lasting and fruitful.

According to his data, boys who grew up with a younger sister and then marry a girl who grew up with an older brother have fewer divorces and more children than boys who marry a girl who was the older sister with no brothers at all. In general, Toman suggests that someone who comes from a large family has better luck socially. In seeking to marry someone who duplicates one of the several relationships he has had by growing up in a large family, such a person has more chances at finding a compatible mate. Perhaps Freud and Adler and some of the habit theorists are correct in saying that the structures of the early years are carried into later life. If so, Toman has begun to unravel some of the intricacies, and this information may become very valuable, especially in cultures with small families.

ACHIEVEMENT NEEDS

One of the most far-ranging topics of social psychology today is the formation and function of the human need for achievement—if indeed, it is a single need. David McClelland and John W. Atkinson have led the research on this issue, and have used just about every research technique available to social psychology, from measures of fantasy to controlled experiments, from phenomenological hunches to mathematical models, and sometimes all of these together.[38]

[37] W. Toman, "The Duplication Theorem of Social Relationships as Tested in the General Population," *Psychological Review* 78, no. 5 (September 1971): 380–90.

[38] D. C. McClelland, *The Achieving Society* (New York: Van Nostrand Reinhold, 1961).

David McClelland believes that achievement need can best be measured by using the Thematic Apperception Test. Providing his subject with some of the Thematic Apperception Test pictures he records the stories the subject makes up about the pictures. These stories are then analyzed by counting the occurrence of themes that pertain to "trying to do well with regard to standards of excellence." Athough this measure is not ideally precise from a technical point of view, it has generated a great deal of related research as well as a series of alternative methods of measurement. McClelland argues that his technique measures the degree to which a person attempts to do well for a feeling of accomplishment, and that those who strive for success because they want to do well can be distinguished from those who do well merely for money or recognition.

Some of the research on this achievement need focuses on its development. Appearing very early in a child's life, the achievement need is fairly well developed by the age of eight or ten. Marian R. Winterbottom has pointed out that it occurs more frequently and strongly in families that encourage children to be independent and self-reliant at an early age.[39] Such children are expected to tie their own shoes early in life, or to fix their own bikes, or to prepare their own breakfasts.

Bernard Rosen and Roy D'Andrade went into the homes of boys high in achievement need and boys low in achievement need.[40] They discovered that mothers and fathers of boys with high achievement need set higher goals for their sons in experimental tasks and reacted more positively to their sons' performance than did the parents of boys with low achievement needs. Most interestingly, however, mothers of the high-need boys were more domineering than the mothers of the low-need boys, while the high-need fathers were less domineering than were the low-need fathers. In short, fathers help produce a strong achievement motive in boys if they set high goals and are warm and positive about their sons' performances, and then encourage the boys to exercise their own initiative.

In our discussion of culture and personality in Chapter 7 we shall talk about the implications for a society with a large number of people having high achievement needs. Considering achievement needs is an exciting area of social psychology, one that points to another, and very important, social process—economic development—that is partly based on socialization.

[39] See I. L. Child, "Socialization," in *Handbook of Social Psychology*, ed. G. Lindzey (Reading, Mass.: Addison-Wesley, 1954), vol. 3, pp. 655–92.

[40] B. C. Rosen and Roy D'Andrade, "The Psychological Origins of Achievement Motivation," *Sociometry* 22, no. 3 (September 1959): 185–218.

In Perspective

We have discussed some of the factors that appear to be involved in the socialization of people and we have looked at some of the products of socialization. Socialization certainly does not end with childhood but continuously shapes and molds people throughout their lives. Some of the effects of early pressures and experiences are lifelong; others are shortlived and become overlaid by new learnings or new requirements that the public and private settings of our lives place upon us. But we probably change less easily as time passes and experiences pile up. Each person develops stronger traits and more subtle defenses just at the time that it becomes harder for other persons to take over from the family and exert the massive control needed to use the processes of imitation, identification, and vicarious reinforcement in a tendentious manner. Socialization, then, is a huge process that we only partially understand, having, as we do, only bits of information about its nature. But the evidence we do have suggests that the general process of socialization will some day rank with genetic endowment and personal development as one of the formative forces of human beings, creating both differences and similarities.

We must recognize, however, that a great deal of our knowledge about socialization of personality comes from America and from other countries of Western civilization. This is both understandable and useful to us, but our intellectual ethnocentrism is beginning to crumble under the impact of the growth of social psychology in other world areas. Furthermore, American social psychologists more and more are beginning comparative studies as they work in other cultures.

We outlined some pan-cultural dimensions that underlie differences in the handling of children earlier in this chapter. These factors emerged after a study of socialization practices in six widely different areas of the world. This costly research procedure was undertaken because of an awareness of the great differences in those practices that shape people to conform to the values of those around them.

We shall therefore return, in our last chapter, to the socialization process in our search for an understanding of the broad issue of how personality is related to culture and society. On a world scale we shall see the shape of the general socialization process most clearly, and a world perspective is now emerging in social psychology.

Before tackling global problems, however, we must look still more closely at the fine texture of social behavior. To begin, in the next chapter we shall focus on the ubiquitous process of perceiving and judging the social world, keeping in mind, as we must, that each person's socialization contributes to, and is greatly affected by, the particular form and content of the momentary social situations, tasks, and roles in which he finds himself.

Perceiving and Judging Social Events

chapter three

So far we have concentrated on large-scale, diffuse social influences—identification, aggressiveness, compliance, conscience. Now we want to direct attention to the finer aspects of how human beings cope with their social world. Our main theme in this chapter will be how people use the information immediately available in social situations in perceiving and interpreting those situations. Since socialization, of course, determines in part how people use such information, we cannot bypass personality determinants. Still, our purpose here is to examine the shorter-term mechanisms of social perception. In general terms, our aim is to describe what is known about how social information is *received* (that is, how social stimuli are interpreted) as well as how social information is *sent* (either intentionally or unintentionally).

But first we have to face up to certain difficulties. The same physical-social information can often be interpreted in a number of ways. The noises of a cocktail party betoken joy to one person, fear to another. A pleasant grin on the face of a friend is satisfying to one person but a disappointment to someone who hoped to see a much broader sign

photo by Pierre Gaudard

of welcome. There are, then, many ways the same stimulus situation can be *received*. In research on physical-social information, equating or systematically varying the motivations and habits of subjects is necessary for evaluating the influence of the immediately present information on subjects' percepts and judgments. For example, the murmur of voices at a party may *always* be pleasant to any new arrival. But this common pleasantness may be lost because it disappears into the welter of other unknown or uncontrolled feelings and wishes the new arrival brings with him.

Similarly, there may be many ways to send information in order to achieve the same perception or judgment. You can make someone feel rejected in a number of different ways. There are also various ways for a boy to prove that he is a bright, ambitious, all-American male. The various ways of sending information raises problems for research in social psychology. In the pages that follow, we will often be reporting on only *some* of the informational conditions that affect most people in a particular way, or on *some* of the conditions under which particular information is sent. We are not yet able to be exhaustive in this field—we simply lack the knowledge to do so.

It is worth noting, also, that the conditions for accurately receiving information are often very different from the conditions for sending the same information. Although you may spot the movements and intonations that mean someone is about to criticize you, these movements or intonations have little to do with the person being critical in the first place. In the following examples we will keep separate the conditions of *perceiving* X from the conditions for *sending* X, although both are of interest to social psychologists.

ON THE FAILURE OF PERCEPTION

Social psychologists Eunice Cooper and Marie Jahoda have prepared some cartoons featuring a "Mr. Biggot," which lampoon bigotry.[1] It is doubly (and rather frighteningly) humorous, however, when an extremely bigoted observer sees the cartoons as upholding bigotry rather than satirizing it! Indeed a person's failure to perceive social events accurately usually strikes us as being funny. Often, too, such failures are sad—even tragic—as when a well-intentioned sheriff is not sensitive enough to prevent an angry group from turning into a lynch mob.

A practical joker enjoys placing others into unperceived or unexpected situations. Similarly, a manipulator of a mob, the leader of a political power play, a person who aims to break a horse—all have the same general intent: to engineer a change so that it is not perceived in time, or at all, by the one being manipulated. The mob is aroused by quiet, vicious rumors so that the sheriff will not see the growing anger. The power of the opposition is cut away by secret negotiation until the final vote so that the actual state of affairs will not be recognized. The horse is imperceptibly lured to compliance as gradually heavier things are loaded on his back (cloth, then blankets, then a saddle, finally a man) before his vigilance against change can be aroused.

Social psychologists are interested in the everyday conditions that lead to both accurate and inaccurate judgment of social events. They are also interested in states of emotion in others, people's intentions,

---

[1] E. Cooper and M. Jahoda, "The Evasion of Propaganda: How Prejudiced People Respond to Anti-Prejudice Propaganda," *Journal of Psychology* 23 (1947): 15–25.

and the perceptions people have of hierarchical social orders in their groups.

THE PROBLEM OF PERCEPTION

Our perceptions are sometimes treated by researchers as very special and mysteriously private occurrences that have to do with what we *really* see, hear, or feel, as different from what we *do about* the things we see, hear, or feel. In fact, some people may argue that we should talk of perception only when the event or object being perceived is actually present to the perceiver, and refer to another process—cognition, for example—when the observer is judging or recalling some object or event of the recent past. We shall use the term *perception* more loosely to include cognition as well.

Perceptions of social events, in fact, may not be a special class of occurrences. Donald Campbell has recently suggested a very close tie between how we see something and what we do about it.[2] In fact, "how I see" something may merely be an alternative way of reporting "what I am about to do." When we report that atomic war is threatening we are also stating that we are prepared to act and vote to avoid war. When a football coach bulwarks his line to counter the opponent's right end, he is thereby displaying his perception of the qualities of the opposing team. Perceiving is, then, a way of acting that has close relations to other ways of acting.

For research purposes, therefore, we consider that a subject has perceived an object when he consistently *talks or otherwise acts* differently in that object's presence (or recent presence) under conditions where the researcher has independently checked or varied the presence of that object. For example, a clever experimenter can alter the informal structure of a group by adding to it a very dominating person. He can check the perception of this change by either noting consistent (and reasonable) changes in the behavior of the other members of the group, or by asking these members to make verbal statements about the changed relations in the group. Some insensitive members may not notice change and not act differently; others may immediately detect that a new social event has occurred and behave accordingly.

The great challenge in this kind of research is how to achieve control over the occurrence of a social event so that the conditions of its perception can be studied. Such control calls for much ingenuity and,

---

[2] D. Campbell, "Social Attitudes and Other Acquired Behavioral Dispositions," *Psychology: A Study of a Science*, ed. S. Koch (New York: McGraw-Hill, 1963), vol. 6.

increasingly, much use of new equipment and social illusion on the part of the researchers. Yet creating even the apparent occurrence of social events—even with the best equipment and the boldest use of illusion—is limited. It is almost impossible to create the actual occurrence of some social events. For instance, it is dangerous to try to cause mobs to form, or rebellions to arise in a small group, or human trust to be undermined. And we can hardly begin to create even the illusion of a revolution. It becomes evident that our research in social perception has barely begun, particularly when we see that we must systematically vary the occurrence of a social event in order to discover what information is necessary to enable the average person to perceive the event.

Great individual differences exist in the speed and accuracy of spotting a social event or a change in a situation because such judgments rest to so great a degree on past learning. Thus, it is difficult in a research setting to decide when a quick spotting of a social event results from the information being varied by the experimenter or from old habits of attention of the subject. The rebellious son of a dominating father may see the dominating quality of a new group member at once. The trouble is that he may see *any* new member as dominating, or he may overreact to obvious dominance but may be blind to subtle forms of manipulation.

The exciting research by Stanley Schachter comparing obese to "normal" (non-obese) people exemplifies and deepens our grasp of how we perceive social events.[3] Obese people tend to react by eating *more* than normals do when the cues of food are prominent, but they eat *less* than normals do when the cues of food are less prominent. Indeed, data suggest that obese people are *generally* more controlled by prominent external stimuli than are normals, who respond more to internal information (like hunger). The basic causal sequence here is still not explicit, although there is a fascinating parallel between the perception and reactivity of these obese people and the way rats with certain hypothalamic brain lesions respond to information. We still lack direct evidence of hypothalamic involvement in human obesity, however, Schachter's work is not essentially a study of perception or judgment, but rather it has to do with differential and sometimes delayed effects of perception upon the eating habits of obese as compared to normal people.

Jerome Singer and David Glass have highlighted the delayed effects of perceived laboratory noise pollution.[4] In their experiments, even loud

[3] S. Schachter, *Emotion, Obesity, and Crime* (New York: Academic Press, 1971).

[4] D. Glass, and J. Singer, *The Urban Condition: Its Stress and Adaptation* (New York: Academic Press, 1972).

noise does not directly affect the subject's performance on a task. Noise, however, produces indirect and delayed effects so that individuals who have worked through a loud noise are less prone to volunteer to work in later experiments. But reducing noise level was less effective in cutting out these aftereffects than providing a switch so that subjects had voluntary control over the noise. The perception of having control (so as to *choose* to work with noise present) cut down aftereffects even when the subjects didn't use the switch! We may conclude therefore, that one form of perception (in this case, control) wards off the negative effects of another (noise).

Despite these complexities, our interest here is to report some attempts to discover the information *anybody* needs to spot social events. Much research energy has been applied to uncovering the way individuals' past learning, needs, and biases affect their use of social information. Our discussion will touch on examples of internal sources of judgments, but we will concentrate mainly on cases that may cast light on the conditions for accurate social judgments, or relevant ensuing action.

THE PERCEPTION OF THE LINE OF REGARD

The direction of a person's glance can be a social event. Although it seems simple enough, the direction of glance can play a critical role in interpersonal behavior. In games and sports the direction of a person's eyes may give away his next action. Children are extremely sensitive to being looked at and rhesus monkeys register a change in electrical potential from the brain stem when people look at them.

Looking at someone is an observable action that can be easily engineered for experimental purposes. James Gibson and Ann Danielson trained a woman to place her eyes precisely in any of seven positions relative to an observer, and to place her head in any one of three positions.[5] One of the eye positions was a fixation on the middle of the observer's forehead and one of the head positions was that of directly facing the observer. The "looker" (who, it is reported, had "very large brown eyes") kept her face impassive to prevent incidental cues. Each subject was then asked to state (for all these positions of head and eye, randomly varied) whether he was being looked at directly. Despite poor illumination, subjects made very few errors; in fact, their acuity in judging the looker's line of regard was at least equal to their ability in discriminating fine print on a visual acuity chart. Of course, more errors were made when the line of regard was askance, as when the looker's

[5] J. Gibson and A. D. Pick, "Perception of Another Person's Looking Behavior," *American Journal of Psychology* 76, no. 3 (1963): 386–94.

face was pointed to the left while her eyes were fixed on the forehead of the subject.

Note here the difference between the conditions for *receiving* information about being looked at and those for *sending* the information "I am looking at you." Many Americans who have "skoaled" in true Scandinavian fashion feel some embarrassment when they are first called upon to hold the line of regard mutually with a person of the opposite sex while each finishes a drink. They must learn to control an act (looking at another) that is usually left to expressive spontaneity. Or is it?

Ralph Exline has begun to study some of the conditions under which this "mutual visual interaction" occurs apparently spontaneously.[6] He first measured 48 subjects for their usual spontaneous tendency to gaze into another's eyes. Then he retested them after they had been embarrassed by being implicated in cheating while working jointly with another person, who was a confederate of the experimenter. While being interrogated about this event, subjects tended to look directly at the interrogator less often than they had before. However, subjects whose answers to a questionnaire showed them to be high on Machiavellianism looked away far less between tests than did those who were low on Machiavellianism. A high Machiavellianism score means that a person is more ready than most to manipulate other people for practical ends.[7] Thus the traits of a person must be taken in conjunction with the situation of the embarrassing interrogation in future predictions of whether he will spontaneously gaze eye-to-eye with another person.

It would be instructive to investigate whether people who make the most errors in receiving information about another's line of regard are low Machiavellians who may have had less practice in staring at others. Our main point should be clear, however: In studying the conditions for receiving a certain kind of information (like being looked at) it is fruitful as well to study the conditions for sending that same information (looking at another, or looking mutually at one another), since both occur, sometimes simultaneously, in everyday life. And the conditions for sending information may be closely related with the conditions for receiving information.

Adam Kendon and Mark Cook have begun to study the conditions for sending "looks" at others in a conversation as well as how these looks are perceived or judged by the recipient.[8] Devising measures of

[6] R. Exline et al., "Visual Interaction in Relation to Machiavellianism and an Unethical Act," *American Psychologist* 16, no. 7 (July 1961): 396.

[7] R. Christie and F. Geis, *Studies in Machiavellianism* (New York: Academic Press, 1970).

[8] A. Kendon and M. Cook, "The Consistency of Gaze Patterns in Social Interaction," *British Journal of Psychology* 60, no. 4 (1969): 481–94.

gaze and of talking, the researchers found that their (English) subjects were quite consistent in their gazing and talking habits while conversing separately with four different people, although there was some tendency for the conversants to match gaze lengths with each other. The recipients, preferring long infrequent gazes to short frequent ones, reported that the person who uses short frequent gazes (especially while listening) is not liked. Kendon's data suggest that when an interaction is not running smoothly there will be a pattern of long utterance by one subject and short frequent gazes by both. This pattern is more frequently found in subjects with high neuroticism scores. Extroverts generally do more looking while speaking (as well as while listening) and apparently enjoy more the bracing or arousing effects of eye contact.

We have hardly begun to ask the intriguing questions involved in even this simple form of interaction. Gibson, after all, studied just "being looked at"; Exline and Kendon studied "looking into the line of regard of another" or just gazing while talking or listening. But what are the physical and personality conditions under which we send or receive such acts as "peering," "glancing," "glowering," "contemplating," "looking bashfully or covertly," "letting the gaze wander," or simply looking right or left when talking with another person—a new line of study of Paul Bokan.[9]

THE PERCEPTION OF FACIAL EXPRESSION

People usually judge the line of regard in the context of facial expression. What do we know about how we perceive expressions? Photography has provided psychologists with a way to engineer information about faces by systematically varying facial features in pictures. Foam rubber and plastics promise even more flexibility in physically engineering facial expressions, but work has just begun on this approach to the study of what James Gibson calls the "information carried by deformations of rubbery surfaces such as a face."

Pictures are only a beginning in representing the complex actuality of facial expressions we see every day. Through pictures, however, we have recently come to some understanding of what facial expressions are universally understood by human beings. This does not mean that the emotion *observed* is the emotion felt, or that the emotion felt is the one that is *displayed*. In the usual experimental procedure, an observer looks at a picture of a face and either tells what he sees there, or merely rates the photograph on a prearranged scale.

The most popular scale is that of Robert Woodworth, who reduced

[9] P. Bokan, "The Eyes Have It," *Psychology Today* 4 (1971): 64ff.

emotional expression to seven common categories and constructed the following scale:

a) love, happiness, and mirth
b) surprise
c) fear and suffering
d) anger and determination
e) disgust
f) contempt
g) (a residual category)

Woodworth showed that subjects rarely disagreed by more than one category in evaluating the same picture. Harold Schlosberg continued this work, finding that only three dimensions are needed for describing all facial expressions: degrees of pleasantness and unpleasantness, degrees of acceptance and rejection, and degrees of arousal.[10] Harry Triandis and W. W. Lambert found supportive evidence for this view in a rural Greek community, and Arthur Wolf and W. W. Lambert have evidence that villagers in Taiwan and college students at Brown University can read the facial expressions on photographs of an American girl the same way.[11] Although Taiwanese may be trained to display more subtle facial expressions than Americans commonly use, members of both cultures receive facial messages in similar ways.

Work has only begun on the social and personal conditions for *sending* facial expression information spontaneously or in a studied manner the way some actors do. Why do people with diverse cultural backgrounds agree that particular facial patterns show "determination," or that Mickey Mouse (an international star) is "cute"? Is the basis for such common judgments learned through some common experience? Do these judgments depend merely on a cultural stereotype (although the cross-cultural evidence throws some doubt on this possibility)? Or does such cross-cultural commonality in judgments reflect that there are certain unlearned facial expressions all human beings use to express emotions? If this last is true, then Schlosberg's basic dimensions of our actual feeling states may provide us with a theory of emotions per se (as he thinks), as well as a theory regarding the conditions for agreement in the perception of emotions.

[10] H. Schlosberg, "Three Dimensions of Emotion," *Psychological Review* 61 (1954): 81–88.

[11] H. Triandis and W. W. Lambert, "A Restatement and Test of Schlosberg's Theory of Emotion with Two Kinds of Subjects from Greece," *Journal of Abnormal and Social Psychology* 56, no. 3 (May 1958): 321–82; A. Wolf, W. W. Lambert, and C. Otterbein, "A Cross-Cultural and Cross-Population Study of the Dimensions Underlying Judgments of Facial Expressions," unpublished manuscript, Cornell University, 1963.

Forming Impressions of Others

The characteristic ways a person uses his line of regard and his face to express emotions or to send information are socially important in part because they permit one person to form impressions of another's personality. The impressions, in turn, are of practical importance—as every politician or statesman knows—since people use these impressions to predict an individual's future behavior and to determine their own behavior in response.

Research on the formation or reception of impressions is in its infancy but has already produced some developments. For one, Solomon Asch investigated the role of language.[12] He asked subjects to write down their imaginative impressions of a person described as "industrious, skillful, intelligent, warm, determined, practical, cautious." Another group heard the same description with the single change of "cold" in place of "warm." The overall impressions were markedly different between groups; apparently each group organized its pieces of information into a whole, focusing on certain "central" traits (such as warmth and coldness), giving scant attention to "peripheral" traits (such as politeness and bluntness). The final impression is not only more than the sum of its parts but it also cannot be derived or predicted from the separate bits of information provided. It is possible to vary received impressions by careful manipulation of the known centrality or peripherality of the trait words, and much research is underway to fathom how we combine the lists of information received (is it a matter of simple summation or of complicated averaging?)[13] and how we overlook, distort, or change the meaning of inconsistent information.[14] How, for example, would we prepare ourselves to interact with a person described to us as "an intelligent but rebellious Negro doctor from France who is a devoted Catholic?"

Compounded meanings of this sort are recognized as essential aspects of the perceptual process as Fritz Heider has so convincingly demonstrated.[15] Each of us applies our own networks of meanings in form-

[12] S. E. Asch, "Forming Impressions of Personality," *Journal of Abnormal and Social Psychology* 41 (1946): 258–90.

[13] H. C. Triandis and M. Fishbein, "Cognitive Interaction in Person Perception," *Journal of Abnormal and Social Psychology* 67 (November 1963): 446–53.

[14] A. H. Hastorf, D. J. Schneider, and J. Polefka, *Person Perception* (Reading, Mass.: Addison-Wesley, 1970).

[15] F. Heider, *The Psychology of Interpersonal Relations* (New York: John Wiley, 1958).

ing impressions; that is, we transform the impressions meant to be sent in one way to those actually received by us. Our distinctive perceptual styles help some of us see through rose-colored perceptual filters and others through blue ones so that we have quite different percepts or interpretations of the same stimulating configuration. Current research is also directed to understanding how these distinctive filtering systems are shaped in the course of maturation, through socialization or particular interpersonal experiences.[16]

Each item of information, then, contributes to the impression, within the context of what the subject is set to make judgments about. Knowing the information received by the subject *and* what he is set to judge about the other, we can predict the content of his judgment or impression. The wise impression-sender must try to control both these factors. It does little good for an advertiser to show that his soap product is soft and pure if the listener is waiting to judge how strong and effective it is. The experimenter (and to some extent, the advertiser) can control the selective *set* of the subject, but it is more difficult to *predict* what set will occur under everyday conditions. The social psychology of interpersonal perception will advance as subjects' wants, interests, and personal filter systems are studied in detail.

Although Asch-like effects have been shown when people rather than verbal descriptions of people have been used in experimental conditions, research on the total range of information available for impression formation has just begun. Explorations have been made, for instance, into how people can empathize with the feelings and judgments of others. Urie Bronfenbrenner and colleagues found at least two skills, or empathic abilities: sensitivity to the *generalized other*, or the *average* feeling or judgment of a group of persons, and sensitivity to the feelings and judgments of *specific* individuals.[17]

Empathy is a complicated research area fraught with many fascinating pitfalls, especially since subjects may appear to be empathetic when they are actually acting on some other basis than the immediate information received. For example, it is often possible to guess what five randomly-selected people think about some topic without ever having met these people at all, particularly if you know what the general opinion on this topic is. You may be surprisingly accurate in guessing about the individual personalities of, say, five students you have not even met. This better-than-chance performance cannot be due to any

[16] P. F. Secord and C. W. Blackman, *Social Psychology* (New York: McGraw-Hill, 1964).

[17] U. Bronfenbrenner, J. Harding, and M. Gallwey, "The Measurement of Skill in Interpersonal Perception," in *Talent and Society*, ed. D. McClelland et al. (New York: Van Nostrand Reinhold, 1958), chap. 2.

empathic ability aroused by specific information about these specific people. In short, it is difficult to rule out the effects of stereotypes that *happen* to be partly correct and to accurately focus on what information from other sources provides for empathizing or impression formation.[18] Victor Cline, however, is demonstrating how accurate some people can be and how clumsy others can be in forming impressions, beyond relying on stereotypes.[19]

The sending of empathy has not been studied directly as yet, though its practical importance is recognized. How does a person communicate empathy? Some people have control over this ability; they leave others with the distinct impression that they understand and feel akin to them even when they are not in fact empathic. Some leave others cold because they don't convey empathy. The ability to send information about empathy (or even the illusion of it) may underlie the success of a politician, a salesman, or a therapist. Some of this skill may stem from a capacity to act according to a learned conception of an empathic person; some of this skill may result from subtle signals that betoken empathy to *any* human being. In any case, by experimentation we can eventually discover the kinds of information needed for the judgment that "this person understands me." The formula for a good bedside manner, for instance, lies over the next research hill, and as we learn more about the expression of empathy we will be better able to distinguish the phony from the real.

Conditions for Judging Social Events

INTENTIONS

The communication of empathy is a complicated problem; it is simpler to study whether a person is seen as having benevolent or malevolent *intentions*. Alfred Baldwin and Nina Lambert have devised a way of predicting whether another person will be judged malevolent or benevolent.[20] They do so by considering some qualities about the judge, along with the information he receives about some crucial social choices made by the subject to be judged.

Suppose, for example, that you are P and must judge the intention of O when he chooses between certain alternative actions. For instance,

---

[18] L. J. Cronbach, "Processes Affecting Scores on 'Understanding of Others' and 'Assumed Similarity,'" *Psychological Bulletin* 52 (1955): 177–93.

[19] V. B. Cline, "Interpersonal Perception," in *Progress in Experimental Personality*, ed. B. A. Maher (New York: Academic Press, 1964).

[20] A. Baldwin, C. Baldwin, I. Hilton, and N. Lambert, "The Measurement of Social Expectations and Their Development in Children," *Child Development Monograph* Serial 128, vol. 34, no. 4 (June 1969).

O is given a choice between an action that would benefit both him and you (P+ O+) and one that would benefit himself but harm you (P− O+). If he chooses the first (P+ O+), can you be sure he is intending to help you? Suppose he chooses P− O+ over P+ O+? Suppose he chooses P− O+ over P+ O−?

It is possible to predict quite accurately the judgments of college students of the degree of benevolence or malevolence in sixteen such abstract situations, but the prediction requires a rather complicated theory that is based, Baldwin feels, on the "naive" beliefs about the psychology of others that we use in everyday life. In short, *assumptions* that judges use in determining whether O is kind or cruel generally serve as a "cultural code." Americans (and, quite likely, people in other nations) assume, for example, that if the two alternatives are identical (for instance P− O− or P− O−), gives no information about his intention. We also assume that others prefer to benefit rather than harm themselves and that people prefer to choose the alternative that results in the *same* outcomes for both of those who are involved. There is evidence that these assumptions are learned at different ages. For example, the first assumption mentioned above has not been learned by four or five years of age, so a child of that age sees O as benevolent when he chooses between P+ O+ and P+ O+, and malevolent when he chooses between P− O− and P− O−.

This method of research may provide a nice way to discover the bases of differences in our perceptions of different social roles. Is a senator judged more or less benevolent than a father when he (as O) chooses P− O− over P− O−?

Baldwin stresses that *learned codes* assist us in making judgments of the intentions of other people, but direct information about O's choice is also instrumental. Indeed, most judgments of complex social events are interpretations of immediate information in terms of codes learned in other, perhaps earlier, similar situations. Thus does the jury judge the criminal and the sheriff predict the mob. Delineating the cultural or personal codes and specifying the information for consistent (and sometimes even "correct") perceptions and judgments constitutes a complicated and challenging problem for social psychologists.

SOCIAL CAUSALITY

Related to Baldwin's work are the experiments of John Thibaut and Henry Riecken on the judgment of causation.[21] Consider yourself a subject in their experiment. You are a college freshman and you have come

[21] J. Thibaut and H. W. Riecken, "Some Determinants and Consequences of the Perception of Social Causality," *Journal of Personality* 24 (September 1955): 113–33.

to a laboratory where you meet two other persons who, apparently, have also come to participate in a social-psychological experiment. One of them turns out to be a neatly-dressed and poised instructor, the other a rather sloppy and unsophisticated freshman. Actually, they are confederates of the experimenter. You are asked by the experimenter to try to persuade these people to donate blood for a Red Cross drive. You do so by sending notes to the two other people who have been put into another room, supposedly to rule out personal, face-to-face persuasion. Eventually each individual complies with your requests. To the research question "What, in your judgment, brought about the compliance in each case?" the finding is as follows: If you are like most subjects tested, you would decide that the high-status Ph.D. complied because he is a nice person; the freshman did so because he was convinced by the force of your argument. Further, because of your perceptions of why they have complied, you would tend to have a more positive attitude toward the high-status person who complied because he's a nice guy than toward the low-status person who gave in because you forced him. In this situation, in short, the cause of compliance is perceived as *external* to the lower-status person, *internal* to the higher-status one.

Note how in this study one judgment is related to an earlier one; that is, *perceived causality* depends on the *perceived status* of the other person. However, Thibaut and Riecken had trouble in manipulating the situation so that all subjects put the right person in the right status. The two confederates, for the purposes of the experimental control, shifted back and forth from one testing session to another in the roles they played. One was relaxed and soft-spoken, the other more formal and stern. Thus, when the stern actor took the high-status role, status discrimination was easy for the subject; but when the soft-spoken actor took the role, the distinction was not so clearly made since the more authoritative person was trying to play the lowly freshman and the more easy-going person was trying to be a lordly Ph.D. Errors in the perception of status tended to affect the perception of causality in a manner consistent with the main findings of the study.

The practical value of this study is displayed by a follow-up experiment by Lloyd Strickland.[22] Here subjects were to be supervisors of the work of two subordinates who, again, were really confederates of the experimenter in an experiment supposedly on work supervision. The work of both subordinates was equal in all cases, but it was prearranged that the supervisor would have more surveillance over the work of subordinate A than of subordinate B. This had two effects:

[22] L. Strickland, "Surveillance and Trust," *Journal of Personality* 26 (1958): 200–215.

First, the supervisor came to trust subordinate B's motivation to work more than he did subordinate A's. This was because he thought B liked the work for internal reasons ("he is a conscientious person"), whereas A worked *because* he was watched. Second, when given a chance later to watch over these subordinates equally, the subject supervisor *chose* on his own to continue the differential surveillance foisted on him at the beginning.

In the Strickland study, quality of work did not play a role; only the amount of work done was incorporated in the study. When quality of work is introduced, Arie Kruglanski recently found it made a difference: it is only when the supervisor knows that A and B produced the same quantity and quality that he attributes B's performance to internal reasons.[23]

Thibaut and Riecken believe that the principle of social perception involved here has further consequences. They consider what happens when a tyrannical government attempts to get compliance from its citizens. First, the tyrannous leaders may take occasions to push people around. Then, the more they force compliance through external pressure the fewer signs they see of spontaneous, loyal compliance based on affection (internal causality). This judgment leads to more forceful use of power, which, in turn, still further decreases the chance of perceiving spontaneous, secure compliance. And this cycle may go on until rebellion occurs. These principles of social perception may be very important social-psychological ideas indeed!

The studies we have cited deal with the ways we attribute characteristics to other people and to ourselves. In fact, attribution theory is currently one of the most active and exciting studies of social psychology. Whether or not we realize it, in our social interactions we continuously attempt to attribute another person's actions to appropriate causes. As Harold Kelley puts it, the attribution process underlies what prompts or causes such everyday phenomena as a student complimenting a professor's lecture, a friend reneging on his share in a collaborative project, or a professor giving special attention to an individual student.[24] Of course, since our own behavior toward other people contributes to their action, we ourselves play a vital role in the behavior of others we try so hard to fathom.

The tendency to attribute another person's behavior to internal or external causes is one formulation that has resulted from attribution re-

[23] A. Kruglanski, "Attributing Trustworthiness in Supervisor-Worker Relations," *Journal of Experimental Social Psychology* 6 (April 1970): 214–32.

[24] H. H. Kelley, *Attribution in Social Interaction* (New York: General Learning Corp., 1971).

search. Edward Jones and colleagues are conducting research on the factors that control the type of attributions people make. Jones maintains that we are perhaps too prone to find internal causes for another's action.[25] For example, when someone explains with plausible (external) excuses why they did poorly at a game, on an exam, or in a love affair, we may appear to agree while we really attribute the failure to an internal cause—the person may be a born loser. Future studies will go deeper into what factors determine our attribution behavior. For example, the feelings we have for the other person may prove important. When we love someone, we not only believe his or her excuses, but we try to provide better ones. And when we discuss our own failures with others we trust, we are more likely to avoid simple external excuses.

This matter of the perceived locus—internal versus external—of the causes of behavior is an extremely powerful notion. We saw an example of it earlier in the chapter in the work of Glass and Singer. They demonstrated that when a person believes he has internal control over noise pollution, with his own shut-out button that he can activate at will, he can live with noise more effectively and comfortably. N. A. Ferrare takes the same idea an important step further in his 1962 doctoral investigation of elderly people facing the trauma of moving into an old age home. Ferrare's thesis, "Institutionalization and Attitude Change in an Aged Population" (Case Western Reserve University), contrasted two groups of elderly ladies: the women in one group felt they had no choice but to enter the home; those in the second group felt they had various alternatives and entered the home voluntarily. In time it turned out that those who could decide for themselves (internal locus) lived longer and more contentedly than those who had no decision to make (external locus). The feeling that we have a hand in our own destiny, that we have within ourselves a shut-out button to control our lives, may be part of the psychological foundation for hope, health, personal esteem, and freedom. Although this new emphasis in social perception is refreshing, there is nonetheless a serious debate shaping up on this issue. As we shall see in Chapter 5, B. F. Skinner feels that illusions permeate the literature of "freedom and dignity." He proposes a plan to externalize concepts such as esteem, freedom, and dignity so that various factors of psychological well-being can be optimized for all individuals.

However, we must be aware of the problems that lurk in all these experiments. Even when experiments are carefully designed and performed, all human beings do not behave as the principle says that they should. Some subjects fail to see that an instructor with a Ph.D. has

---

[25] E. E. Jones and R. E. Nisbett, *The Actor and the Observer: Divergent Perceptions of the Causes of Behavior* (New York: General Learning Corp., 1971).

more power or status than a freshman has; some subjects do not perceive that the high-status person's compliance is based on internal causes. A few subjects perceive that the high-status person is only giving in because he has been pushed into it. Social psychologists are constantly searching for ways to reduce these exceptions in their data, or of recognizing some of these exceptions as new sources of data in their own right.

Many studies purport to show that a person views those who have influence over him as likeable. Renato Tagiuri and others, however, have thoughtfully pointed out that there are at least four patterns of such relationships:[26]

1. some persons like best those with whom they share mutual influence

2. others like best those they feel that they influence

3. some like best those who influence them

4. some subjects display only a weak relationship between preference and influence.

We must constantly beware of the easy overgeneralizing on behavior as slippery as social perception.

SOCIAL HIERARCHIES

Although cultural and personal codes often help us to make useful or true social discriminations, we do tend to use them inappropriately. At the risk of getting sidetracked into misperception rather than searching out the conditions for accurate perception, let us consider the problems of learning to perceive, judge, and remember *social structures.*

Plainly, real-life social structures come in all shapes and sizes and with diverse relationships holding them together. Let us consider, for the moment, only four-person groups (and let us limit ourselves to four men in order to keep down the usual complexities added by sex differences). In one such group, the *influence structure* may have this pattern: A influences B, C, and D; B influences C and D; and C influences D. In short, a simple chain of command of influence exists, like that in the military. Another group may be the same, except that B has no influence over C and D. Or, again, in another group, A may influence B and vice versa, and C can influence D and vice versa, but there is no influence from one pair to the other. Finally (but by no means exhaustively) the scheme may be $A \rightarrow B \rightarrow C \rightarrow D$, along with $A \rightarrow D$, $D \rightarrow B$, and $C \rightarrow A$. There are vast varieties of such structures in the social

[26] R. Tagiuri and N. Kagan, "Personal Preference and the Attribution of Influence in Small Groups," *Journal of Personality* 28, no. 3 (1960): 257–65.

world, and all of us have met many of them, whether we perceived them or not.

Clinton De Soto has done experiments that suggest that college students are alert to power-based orderings as in the chain-of-command example above.[27] In his experiments, De Soto worked out the possible relations among people involved in these various structures, gave names to A, B, C, and D and wrote each relationship on the back of a card (for example, "Alan influences Bill"). On the front of each card he wrote a question, such as "Does Alan influence Bill or does he not?" The subject's task was to learn the answers to all the questions for each structure in as few trials as possible. The subject first tried to answer each question, then he was permitted to turn the card over to see whether he was correct. De Soto's hypothesis was borne out—the chain-of-command structure was by far the easiest to learn; it took almost three times as many trials for subjects to learn the correct answer to the same number of cards that represented the *last* structure suggested above.

In judging (or learning) influence structures De Soto believes that human beings tend to use a code (or *schema,* as he prefers to call it) that finds order even when it does not exist. With this ordering, structures like the last one above (C → A) may appear to be unnatural. De Soto even suggests that such a code may come to act as a *social expectation.* We expect a group to have a simple pecking order and, if this expectation is shared by others in the group, a pecking order will emerge although there was no previous need for ordering the group. De Soto's suggestion is certainly worthy of further research to investigate the political expectation of people who, like Americans, say that they prefer democratic structures to chain-of-command structures.

We should also report that this tendency toward perceiving simple order does not hold for other aspects of social structures such as relations of confiding and liking. In fact, people tend to expect relations of confidence to be symmetrical: when A confides in B, B will be expected to confide in A.

SOCIAL CONTRIBUTION

A study by Henry Riecken points up the difficulties involved in doing clear research on the judgment of social events as well as the beginnings we are making in solving these difficulties.[28] Riecken investi-

---

[27] C. B. De Soto, "Learning a Social Structure," *Journal of Abnormal and Social Psychology* 60 (May 1960): 417–21; see also De Soto et al., "Balance and the Grouping Schema," *Journal of Personal and Social Psychology* 8 (January 1968): 1–17.

[28] H. W. Riecken, "The Effect of Talkativeness on Ability to Influence Group Solutions to Problems," *Sociometry* 21 (1958): 309–21.

gated how credit is assigned for contributing good ideas in a group discussion. Common experience, confirmed by the results of some early studies, suggests that the talkative group member often gets a good deal of credit from the others, more than he deserves. The earlier studies on this problem kept a reliable, objective record of only one element—talkativeness—which is easy to count, while the actual quality of suggestions made by the talkative people (and others) was left to vary naturally and was measured by the judgments of the group members themselves, not perhaps the most accurate judges.

Riecken devised a means of experimentally varying both the quality of contribution and the contributor. In his experiment, four-man teams discussed case problems in human relations. One such problem had a unique and elegant solution that was hard to discover without help. The experimenter, during the discussion, passed on a hint to either the most talkative member of the group or to the least talkative. The chosen person could then present the hint for discussion and possible acceptance.

When the talkative member offered the hint, the others always accepted it as the best solution, except when the talkative person was not really convinced that the solution was good. When the quiet member offered the hint, the others rarely accepted it unless it got the backing of someone more talkative (usually the *second most* talkative member who often acts in many groups as a specialist in handling personal feelings).

Later, group members were asked to judge who contributed most to the solution of the problem. When the top talker had offered the hint and it was accepted, he got credit for it 82 percent of the time. When the low talker's hint was accepted, he received recognition only 60 percent of the time. Furthermore, the top talker was almost uniformly seen as having contributed more than the low talker. Other data show that the top talker does tend to be more effective in convincing people, although he is no better than the low talker at coping with opposition to his suggestions.

It appears, then, that group members are fairly accurate in judging contributions to a discussion, though there is some bias in giving credit to the heaviest contributor as the best contributor. This judgment may be often true, however, because someone who makes frequent suggestions does manage to get a high-quality idea accepted more often. Most people, in fact, appear to work under the assumption that the frequent talker gives the best ideas. Riecken's work provides an example of judgment based on both immediate information and a set of habits in judging.

Donald Hayes and Leo Meltzer told us that they have been unsuccessful in fully replicating Riecken's study because too many of the student subjects thought the experimenter's hint was a poor solution to the problem the group discussed. The experimenter's hint was his suggestion that a plant worker who held up an assembly line be alternated along the various jobs on the line, thus minimizing his effects as a bottleneck. The college students in the experiment, unaware or unenamored of trade union rules, thought the really elegant solution was to fire the troublesome employee. This disagreement between group members and the experimenters highlights the difficulties in attempting to control social occurrences in studying social perception.

The Riecken study, however, did stretch our experimental grasp by demonstrating how to manipulate the quality of a member's contribution to group discussions. Studies are now underway at a number of research centers to manipulate the talkativeness of the subjects as well. One way this can be done is by secretly letting a subject know that the experimenter, or presumably, though not actually, the rest of the group, thinks he is speaking very well and is making valuable contributions. In this way a quiet person can be encouraged to become talkative and, more humanely perhaps, the talkative ones can be shut up. Once this technique is worked out satisfactorily, experimenters can return to Riecken's problem and systematically vary the group's perception of both the quality and quantity of the contributions.

JUDGMENTS OF MAJORITIES

Consider the worries a group chairman or politician has in trying to estimate which side has a majority on a controversial issue. Research by Leon Levy suggests that college students (and, possibly, other people as well) judge the existence of a majority in rather consistent ways. In a group that split 20–20 on some issue, the students said that a split of 30–10 would betoken a clear majority.[29] The ratio between the size of the needed change and the size of the evenly split group tended to remain constant, particularly with larger groups. Thus, a 200–200 division would have to become a 300–100 split for a clear majority to be perceived.

Levy dug deeper into this matter by using a controversial issue that actively engaged the judges. Judges for and against fraternities were asked to decide how big a difference from 20–20 would be decisive on the issue of permitting fraternities on a campus. He found no differences in judgment as the result of the judges' prior commitment to a pro or con position. This evidence suggests that where the tide of senti-

---

[29] L. H. Levy, "Weber Fraction Analogues in Social Perception," *Perceptual Motor Skills* 11 (1960): 233–42.

ment is running against him an individual appears to perceive this just as readily as does the individual running with the tide.

Still, commitment per se *does* affect the size of difference needed for perception of a majority. When a person is committed to a pro or con position it takes a greater difference from an even split before he sees a majority than when the issue is an abstract one outside his interests. In this light, a political leader or group chairman needs to be rather careful in judging voice votes or a showing of hands. There may be resistance to decisions based on less of a majority than is needed to meet the consistent and shared expectation of what constitutes a majority. Voters also prove harder to fool once they recognize that they share a common assumption about what is needed to achieve a majority.

Although there is some doubt about how constant is the ratio that defines a majority, the main point here for us is that the way has been opened for a quantitative study of a fascinating and complex problem of social perception.[30]

Perception and Conceptualization

We have only been able to touch on a few of the interesting and difficult questions involved in social perception. We have seen, however, that our various everyday judgments are determined in differing degrees by (a) the immediate information available to us in a situation, (b) our assumptions, or habits, of judgments, and (c) our commitments. We have emphasized here the first of these factors because it has often been overlooked in social psychology, and because we are beginning to learn to undertake studies and experiments on it.

However, there is another reason for our present emphasis. We are interested in the relationship between social perception and social thinking. The latter grows out of the former, at least to some extent, and our thinking about social events is sometimes limited by our habits of *attention* to immediate information. By giving direct and repeated attention to complex events we develop lasting concepts and beliefs about social matters in the sense that we learn to perceive more finely and with more flexibility the information that is immediately available. Julian Hochberg has shown that under limited laboratory and classroom conditions *attending behavior* can be predicted and controlled through manipulation of the types and amounts of immediate information available to the

30 J. R. Braun and G. A. Haven, "Weber Fraction Analogues in Social Perception: Further Investigation," *Perceptual Motor Skills* 14 (1962): 282.

Immediate information that determines our everyday judgment

eye.[31] He has also begun to unravel how, as our eyes are drawn from feature to feature of a face or of a social scene, we integrate the information into more complex and subtle higher-order conceptions.[32] But we have much to learn about how attending sharpens our perceptual habits and provides a basis for our rich and often confused social concepts.

Direct repeated attending is, of course, only one way of forming our concepts and assumptions about social events. We also pick up concepts and stereotypes indirectly. A major tradition in social psychology has emphasized this indirect route to concepts and assumptions. Students of George Herbert Mead have made a great deal of his idea that there is a basic, even instinctual process, whereby we take on the

[31] J. Hochberg, "The Psychophysics of Pictorial Perception," *Audio-Visual Communications Review* 10, no. 5 (1962): 49–51.

[32] J. Hochberg, "The Representation of Things and People," in *Art, Perception, and Reality,* ed. E. Gombrich and J. Hochberg, (Baltimore, Md.: Johns Hopkins University Press, 1972).

role of the "other" when we interact with people and that we thereby learn shared social roles indirectly.[33] For the African children studied by Cole and his colleagues, indirect learning of roles is more important than straight instruction.[34] In our own society, little new learning is required for a motorist to interact accurately (that is, in the way he is *expected* to act) with a highway patrolman on first meeting; the motorist has long since learned the role of the policeman and that of the caught speeder as part of his general cultural learning. Our motorist simply finds himself taking the role of the policeman in the situation to infer the policeman's present intentions. To take the role of the other is to be able to behave (at least covertly) from the perspective of the other, and thereby anticipate his next moves. We shall return to Mead's instructive view of taking on the role of the other. For now, our main purpose is to highlight *indirect* sources of social ideas and judgments.

Ragnar Rommetveit of Norway has done research on what he considers the three main stages in developing social concepts through *direct* experience:

1. sensitivity to the social event
2. instrumental discrimination of the concept
3. verbal expression of the concept.[35]

Consider a young lady who arrives in Paris to learn the fashion in women's clothes. With her knowledgeable friends she goes to salons and tries on clothing. Her friends, who have the concept of what is fashionable, tell her whether or not the clothes she tries fit the mode. She slowly begins to grasp the concept. Although she is able to discriminate modish clothes more precisely than before, she cannot yet state clearly at all what makes them *haute couture*. She has merely learned to tell the difference between one style of clothes from another style more sensitively.

The second stage occurs when our visitor, through differential social rewards (her friends' agreements, the lingering eyes of men who see her pass, or subtle criticism when she buys unwisely), learns what to buy and what not to buy. She develops a knack for choosing and judging what is correct. To Rommetveit, she has learned an instrumental, or useful, concept, even though she cannot yet express it verbally.

The final stage of concept attainment occurs when our heroine is able to write home and make general and accurate statements about the latest fashions. She now can describe some of the complexities of

[33] A. Straus, ed., *The Social Psychology of George Herbert Mead* (Chicago: University of Chicago Press, 1956).
[34] M. Cole, J. Gay, J. Glick, D. Sharp, *The Cultural Context of Learning and Thinking* (New York: Basic Books, 1971).

Concept formation

dress length, sleeve design, and waist fitting that are the bases on which she and her friends judge the social fact of this year's fashions. This final stage of concept attainment is valuable indeed, and far more rare than we often think.

We have used the lighthearted example of fashion for purposes of illustration, but it may be that this sequence of events accurately describes our attainment of various concepts. Consider the concept of democracy. Many people try to teach students about democracy, often attempting to teach at the verbal, or reporting third level, skipping the earlier stages. Although the student may learn all the verbal statements associated with the term *democracy,* he may never achieve the sensitivity to identify democracy as a social event, as in stage one, or the instrumental discriminative ability called for in stage two.

But there is more to the story than this, if Rommetveit is correct. He points to some fascinating inconsistencies in the levels at which we hold and use concepts. In one study he found subjects who reported

[35] R. Rommetveit, "Stages in Concept Formation and Levels of Cognitive Functioning," *Scandinavian Journal of Psychology* 1 (1960): 115–24.

both before and after a sequence of experiments that they always chose their friends on the basis of honesty. Yet when actually faced with making friendship choices in the course of the experiment, the subjects chose potential friends for what could only be called intellectual ability. Perhaps, like the subjects, we often entertain one notion about our action at the verbal level ("I chose my friends on their honesty") while we utilize a very different instrumental concept (choosing intelligent friends regardless of their honesty). Because admitting our intellectual snobbery might cause us more anxiety than we can bear, we may forget or suppress this knowledge of our actions and build our self-image around more acceptable concepts like honesty, even when we fail to act on them. Many personality defenses may lie between the concepts we hold for our self-image and those we utilize in making choices. Further research in this area may point up these inconsistencies and show us how to achieve more self-honesty and, along with it, more integrated personalities.

The Perception of Social Roles

Let us return to the concept of social role that is so fashionable in contemporary sociological analysis. Social organizations can be analyzed into roles that are played, or fulfilled, by individuals who are usually replaceable. Pitchers pitch baseballs, batters swing bats at what pitchers pitch. People who pitch also bat. Batters try to play the role of pitchers in order to anticipate the form of the next pitch, as pitchers try to anticipate events from the perspective of the batter, and so on. Of course, the traits, moods, and attitudes of actors help create great individual differences in the ways roles are played, but overall role structure is largely invariant, regardless of individuals. Edgar Borgatta has made this point clearly.[36] He asked a small group of shy persons and forward persons to play the roles of both a shy policeman and a dominant policeman. The dominant persons played less shy "shy policemen" than did the shy persons, while the shy persons produced less dominant "dominant policemen" than did the dominant ones. But neither group had trouble in producing behavior appropriate to the given roles.

We all learn to judge more or less accurately the appropriateness of the behaviors of people who play many common roles around us. We all feel quite assured in saying, "He's not acting like a proper father, [or senator, or liberal]." Furthermore, we are apparently able to dis-

[36] E. Borgatta, "Role Specification and Personality," (Mimeographed report, Cornell University, 1961).

criminate even the more subtle roles, as when we look for leadership to the most productive group member in getting a job done, but turn to a different person when we have a gripe or need to be reassured. We may not even have terms for such a difference in role (say, "task leader" or "social leader") since the concepts underlying our different behavior toward them have not developed to Rommetveit's third stage (accurate verbal expression of the concept). Yet we are able to spot the apparent effects of a role that have rubbed off on a person even when he is not actually in the role. A retired general acts like a general still, and a policeman on vacation often gives himself away by the things he pays attention to or his special attitudes.

The perception of roles and role effects is a complex and sophisticated case of social perception, representing an integration of all the processes discussed in this chapter. Our assumptions about a person in a role cover his feelings and his emotional expressions ("a diplomat should at least appear to be cool and collected"); his motivations and traits ("Caesar's wife should be, at or least appear to be virtuous"); his intentions ("a good cop should be helpful to kids, or at least make the kids think he is"); his contribution to a social situation ("a good senator suggests new laws"); and his position in a social hierarchy ("politicans are big shots in our town"). All these—and many other as yet unstudied— facts of social perception will help cast light on role perception on which accurate social behavior depends. The more intimate, lengthy, and important our interaction with others is, the more differentiated and accurate our role judgments become, so that more aspects of the other person, his performance, and the situational setting become relevant in deciding our own response to him.

A role is, then, a complex social act, and recently social psychologists have become interested in the principles by which people master the complexity of role judgment. How do the parts coalesce into a unified role impression? Harry Triandis and Martin Fishbein have concentrated on how beliefs and evaluations of separate role items determine the final evaluation of a cluster of these items.[37] Knowing a subject's beliefs and evaluations about Negroes and coal miners, for instance, the experimenter's problem is to predict how the subject will evaluate "a Negro coal miner." This is a fairly simple task. The technical difficulty is greater, of course, when we attempt to predict from knowledge about the various components the resultant evaluation of "Negro Portuguese coal miner of different religion from yours." Evaluations of the parts as predictors of the evaluation of the total tap only a limited segment

[37] H. C. Triandis and M. Fishbein, "Cognitive Interaction in Person Perception," *Journal of Abnormal and Social Psychology* (November 1963): 446–53.

of role perception, although there is more to perception than the judgment of value.

Consider a subject who likes Negroes but hates coal miners. The most fashionable theories in social psychology—those called balance, or consistency, theories—would all predict that he would evaluate a "Negro coal miner" somewhere on a scale *between* his liking for Negroes and his dislike for coal miners. Such a resolution would provide a balance in his thoughts and would provide the congruity most people prefer rather than the incongruity from associating two incompatible terms.

Using role descriptions, Triandis and Fishbein analyzed the judgments of a number of subjects from Greece and the United States. They found at once that for both Greeks and Americans the *occupational component* in such a role description as "Negro Portuguese coal miner of a different religion from yours" is the most powerful component in forming the total judgment. The next most important component for the Greeks was religion; for the Americans it was race.

Theoretically, however, Triandis and Fishbein's most interesting discovery was that the balance theory, although it predicted the judgment of the composites fairly well, did not operate as effectively as what they call the *cognitive summation principle*. In the balance theory the value of the complex role is related to the *mean*, or *average*, of the scaled value of the components; in the theory using the cognitive summation principle the composite judgment is related to the *sum*, or *total*, of the scaled values of each component, weighted according to their cultural prominence (as in the case of the occupational component above). In balance theory two favored items put together would never be evaluated higher than the more favored of the two; in Fishbein's theory two well-favored items put together could produce a composite that is even more favored than either component. The whole, in short, is more like the sum of the values of the parts than like some point *in between* the values of the parts.

An important advance in role perception research has been made by Frances Aboud and Donald Taylor in Canada.[38] They asked separate groups of English- and French-speaking students to judge *role* concepts ("student," "teacher," or "male," "female") *ethnic* concepts ("English-Canadian," and "French-Canadian") as well as the combinations (e.g., "English-Canadian male"). What is especially interesting is that role stereotypes were used more in judging in-group combinations (e.g.,

[38] F. E. Aboud and D. M. Taylor, "Ethnic and Role Stereotypes: Their Relative Importance in Person Perception," *Journal of Social Psychology* 85 (January 1971): 17–27.

"French-Canadian student" for a French-Canadian subject) whereas ethnic stereotypes predominated in judging out-group combinations. These researchers argue convincingly that since most of our social interactions occur in the context of roles, the tendency to emphasize roles in making intra-group judgments enhances the efficiency of intra-group interactions. The emphasis on ethnic stereotypes in making out-group judgments, however, can hamper interaction in cross-cultural contexts.

Harry Triandis and his associates are developing tools to simplify the study of role judgments.[39] Much effort has gone into uncovering a set of dimensions that underlie such judgments, a set that is valid in more than one culture. At least five such dimensions (having to do with superordination and subordination, association and dissociation, level of activity, level of hostility, and intimacy–formality) are under active consideration. The aim is to discover dimensions of a *role space,* which can be used as we use height, weight, width, and depth to describe rooms and placement of objects in rooms. Given these dimensions, it becomes possible to "place" in the coordinates of the resulting role space the strengths of shared expectations for behavior that each member of a role pair (such as a foreman and laborer, a father and son) bring to their interaction with each other. It is even possible to show where misunderstandings are likely to arise in a family, or across cultural barriers, as when a Greek laborer meets an American foreman. Evidence suggests that the Greek worker will expect a foreman to show personal interest and to pry into his personal affairs. An American worker would expect his foreman to be more distant. Further, the Greek worker will expect to behave himself more formally and with more free expression of hostility than the American is used to. Therefore the Greek worker will see his American boss as cold and distant, the foreman will see the worker as hostile, and both will react with predictable further misunderstanding. Hopefully these researches will point up ahead of time where trouble is likely to occur so that all concerned can be forewarned and forearmed.

In Perspective

This chapter has documented how our accurate perceptual behavior rests upon the immediately available information about the social event.

---

[39] H. Triandis et al., *The Analysis of Subjective Culture* (New York: John Wiley, 1972), and Triandis et al., "Role Perception, Behavioral Intentions, and Perceived Social Behaviors: Three Cross-Cultural Studies of Subjective Culture," in *Comparative Perspectives in Social Psychology,* ed. W. Lambert and R. Weisbrod (Boston: Little, Brown, 1971), pp. 185–213.

Related to, and usually aroused by, such immediate cues, however, are more or less complex associational and cognitive *mediators,* such as cultural codes, that help to interpret the information provided by the social event itself. Thus, there are invariant relationships between eye and head placement that are related to the judgment of being looked at. There are three dimensions of judgment that help to order the information from other people's faces and thus read their emotions. A more or less complex set of assumptions helps us to sort out other people's decisions in making choices so that we can arrive at judgments of their intentions. When someone agrees with us we assess the cause according to our judgment of his relative status, assigning the agreement to *his* personal qualities (internal factors) if he is above us, and to *our* arguments (external factors) if he is below us. We are influenced by the usual talkativeness of others when we assign credit for social contributions. Many situations are perceived according to our personal or socially shared concepts of what is expected of a person in a role. We tend to assume that hierarchies of people are ordered simply until we learn otherwise (if we ever do).

The study of social perception has been held back by the technical troubles that arise when we try to systematically vary the occurrence of social events, but a start has been made. A study of the issues involved in the communication of social and personal cues, along with the reception of such cues, is also underway.

The problem of the perception of persons in roles and the question of how the observer integrates the complex evaluations and other information involved in role perception has been pointed up as a central issue in the study of the perception of social events.

The Social Significance
of Attitudes

chapter four

Suppose you were phoning a local doctor for a first appointment. As you give him the symptoms that prompted the call and hear the doctor's reactions, you are reassured about his competence and kindness. But then suppose a friend should say, "Oh, yes, that's the Chicano doctor who just moved here." If you happen to be a white American, would this extra characteristic affect your state of mind? What if you happen to be a Chicano and had not picked up any ethnic cues in the doctor's speech? According to the ongoing research of Bruce Fraser in Boston and Richard Tucker in Montreal, the doctor's ethnic background would very likely make an important difference to most people.[1] The non-Chicano person's stereotyped attitudes toward Chicanos might well get in the way and change his perspective and, similarly, a Chicano in this situation could be affected by his attitude towards Chicanos who speak without an identifiable accent. Related studies conducted in Great Britain by Howard Giles make it clear that this type of reaction is uni-

[1] B. Fraser, "Some Unexpected Reactions to Various American-English Dialects," (Mimeographed, Linguistics Department, Harvard University, 1972), G. R. Tucker and W. E. Lambert, "White and Negro Listeners' Reactions to Various American-English Dialects," *Social Forces* 47 (1969): 463–68.

photo by Pierre Gaudard

versal.[2] In England, if the doctor spoke with a Somerset or a Scottish accent his patient would have less confidence in him than if he spoke with a high-prestige "R.P." (Received Pronunciation) English accent. At the same time, though, the R.P. doctor would not be expected to have warmth and good-heartedness.

At what age do attitudes start to show themselves in behavior? To get an idea, Margaret Birks worked with children from five to twelve years old.[3] Protestant youngsters were asked "What do you think Jews are like?" and their responses were analyzed for prejudice. At five years of age, none expressed prejudice or discrimination, while at ten years twenty-seven percent did. And by the age of ten, the children were clearly showing discrimination by excluding Jewish children from their groups of friends. The same development was noted in other large American cities. Starting in the fifth grade, children of Italian background typically choose other Italians as friends, and Jewish children choose other Jews as friends.[4] What underlies these predictable changes in perspectives of others as children grow older and how do these changes get started?

[2] H. Giles, "Patterns of Evaluation in Reactions to R.P., South Welsh and Somerset Accented Speech," *British Journal of Social and Clinical Psychology* 10 (1971): 280–81.

[3] M. Birks, "Discrimination Among Jewish and Protestant Children" (unpublished M.A. thesis, McGill University, 1957).

[4] See J. H. Criswell, "A Sociometric Study of Race Cleavage," *Archives of Psychology*, no. 236 (1939).

In this chapter we focus sharply on one very special form of adjustment—the development of attitudes. The nature and function of attitudes has been a major concern of social psychologists over the years because it is complex, interesting, and has tremendous social significance. The examples just given touch on *prejudiced* attitudes. We shall use prejudice as one of our principal examples of attitudes because its social significance has prompted a great deal of theory and research, and because prejudice highlights the essential components in all attitudes. First, we will define what we mean by *attitudes* and describe their general characteristics, and then we will demonstrate with specific research examples how attitudes are measured. Then we shall illustrate how attitudes affect and shape our behavior and personalities and vice versa. Finally, we shall explain (as well as we can with the facts now known) how attitudes are formed and how they can be changed.

The Nature of Attitudes

An attitude is an organized and consistent manner of thinking, feeling, and reacting to people, groups, social issues or, more generally, to any event in the environment. The essential components of attitudes are thoughts and beliefs, feelings or emotions, and tendencies to react. We can say that an attitude is formed when these components are so interrelated that specific feelings and reaction tendencies become consistently associated with the attitude object. Our attitudes develop in the course of coping with and adjusting to our social environments. Once attitudes are developed, they lend regularity to our modes of reacting and facilitate social adjustment. In the early stages of attitude development, the components can be modified by new experiences. Later, however, their organization may become inflexible and stereotyped, usually because we have been encouraged over long periods of time to react in standard ways to particular events or groups. As an attitude becomes firmly set, we become too ready to categorize people or events according to emotionally toned patterns of thoughts so that we fail to recognize individuality or uniqueness. Fixed or stereotyped attitudes reduce the potential richness of our environments and constrict our reactions.

We are not fully conscious of most of our attitudes nor are we aware of the extensive influence they have on our social behavior. But if we analyze ourselves closely we can learn to detect the functioning of selected, powerful attitudes. If an individual has developed a strong negative or positive attitude towards communism, for example, he considers and evaluates any action by communists or anticommunists in a stereotyped fashion. On careful self-analysis, he can actually sense his reactions of suspicion or hatred (or pride and identification) as he hears about their activities. Similarly, when a new acquaintance turns out to have the same views as we do toward various social issues, we can sense the growth of favorable feelings towards him.

Through introspective glimpses of attitudes functioning with ourselves, we become sensitive to attitudes in others. In fact, we spend a good deal of energy in social interaction trying to figure out the attitudes of others. But people do not openly reveal their attitudes. Through social experience they learn to keep certain of their attitudes hidden from casual acquaintances, or even from close friends. Because this seems to be the typical strategy, we have used the term *reaction tendency* rather than *reaction* for the third component of attitudes to indicate that attitudes are not necessarily overtly expressed. Because of this, success in social interaction often depends on one's skills at inferring the others' thoughts, feelings, and reaction tendencies from subtle behavioral cues.

It is a common human characteristic to make inferences about the attitudes of others and to regulate one's own actions accordingly. From small and limited samples of another's behavior we may conclude, say, that he is liberal, understanding, or unprejudiced, and then react to him in what we consider to be an appropriate manner. Although we all make such inferences, we differ in our capacity to make accurate inferences. The socially sensitive person is skillful at making accurate inferences. Some of us, in fact, are so sensitive to the attitudes of others that we are socially incapacitated. On the other hand, the socially clumsy person frequently misses or misreads the available cues and makes incorrect inferences about another's attitudes because his own attitudes get in the way. Thus, having convinced himself that his views are the only logical ones, he may incorrectly assume that others share his own prejudices. But even the socially clumsy person can learn to recognize the consistency of another's ways of reacting and make reliable inferences about attitudes. He can, for example, profit from experiences with friends. Close friends who are free to discuss differences of thoughts and feelings about mutually important subjects teach each other how to make more accurate estimates of each other's attitudes.

The Measurement of Attitudes

Social psychologists have developed a number of systematic techniques for inferring and measuring attitudes. If a measuring instrument is to be useful, it must, of course, reliably register variations in quantities so that the measured elements can be compared and placed in an order. Devices to measure attitudes, like other instruments, are tested and reworked until they reliably reflect degrees of favorable or unfavorable attitudes. Special problems, however, crop up with such psychological measuring devices. Because people and their attitudes sometimes change from one time period to another, it is difficult to determine a device's reliability. Furthermore, it is not possible to make direct measurements of complex psychological processes such as attitudes. Because most people give incomplete, superficial, and often distorted descriptions of their attitudes, psychologists must be as ingenious as possible to infer the existence and characteristics of an attitude from often camouflaged information about a person's thoughts, feelings, and reaction tendencies. The indirect inferences made about attitudes require careful testing for validity—that is, attitude measures must actually gauge what they are supposed to and not some other psychological process.

Although the information for inferring attitudes can be obtained by systematically observing people in specially created social situations, such an approach takes a great deal of time and feels unnatural for those being observed. Thus psychologists have developed substitute procedures. In the typical case, respondents are asked to imagine themselves in specific social settings and to provide information about their thoughts, feelings, and likely ways of behaving in such settings. As early as 1925 Emory Bogardus asked subjects to imagine themselves in various types of social contact with immigrants (say, Chinese immigrants) and to indicate whether they would like to have them as very close friends, as neighbors, or as colleagues.[5] The situations ranged from acceptance as a marriage partner to rejection even as visitors to one's country. Bogardus's social distance scale permitted an ordering of respondents in terms of their reaction tendencies. Thus, some would agree to accept Chinese as neighbors, while others, showing less concern about social distance, would accept Chinese as potential close friends or marriage partners. (Whether respondents would do so in actual social contexts would depend on the permissiveness of the setting itself and the intensity of the reaction tendencies.) The Bogardus scale has been useful in attitude research, in spite of its limitations: it doesn't provide an index of degree or intensity of reaction tendencies, nor does it obtain information about the thoughts and feelings of respondents. Techniques developed more recently incorporate all three attitude components and insure that variations in each of these is assessed.[6]

[5] E. S. Bogardus, "Measuring Social Distance," *Journal of Applied Sociology* 9 (1925): 299–308.

[6] See H. Triandis, *Attitude and Attitude Change* (New York: John Wiley, 1971).

Let us follow through two examples of how social psychologists go about measuring attitudes. Suppose we were interested in determining the attitudes of Americans towards recent immigrants. Planning the study so that communities of different size could be compared, we might work on the hunch that residents of large cities would be less sensitive than those in small communities to the presence of immigrants. We might also argue in advance that sensitivity towards immigrants would be particularly evident in those who risk losing their jobs to new competition, or in those who live in neighborhoods the immigrants would most likely move into. Questions about these matters could be answered by selecting representative samples of respondents from different socio-economic backgrounds and from different neighborhoods in each community to be studied. At a more personal level, we might anticipate that those with unfavorable attitudes towards immigrants might have a general trait of ethnocentrism. To have information to test such an idea, we could include standard measures of ethnocentrism and generalized prejudice.

Suppose we decided to use a questionnaire method for measuring attitudes towards immigrants, and to make comparisons to *type* (favorable or unfavorable) and *degree* of attitude our major interests. Questionnaire items would then be constructed to represent the three components of attitudes. Respondents would get the opportunity to agree or disagree with each question, thus indicating type of attitude; the intensity of response would be reflected in whether the respondents "agree strongly," "agree," are "uncertain," "disagree," or "strongly disagree." For example, the test items "Generally speaking, I believe immigrants are as trustworthy as anyone else" and "Immigrants seem to have children primarily to send them out to work" permit respondents to express their *thoughts* and *beliefs* about immigrants. The test items "It bothers me the way immigrants stick to their own language and customs" and "I am happy to have my children play with immigrant children" allow expression of *feelings* and *emotions* with regard to immigrants. The items "I would be quite willing to work for an immigrant employer" and "I would likely move out if too many immigrants took homes in my district" allow expression of *reaction tendencies*. If several questions were devised to measure each attitude component, then the *consistency* of the organization of components could be assessed. Furthermore, if half the questions were favorably worded and half unfavorably, we could determine whether an attitude was actually being expressed (in which case, respondents would agree with the questions in one form and disagree with those in the opposite form) rather than a simple tendency to comply (indiscriminately agreeing with any statements, favorable or not).

We would first administer the questionnaire on two different occasions to a test group of representative respondents to determine its *reliability*. The questionnaire would be considered reliable if the questions elicited the same responses on both occasions; we would then eliminate unreliable questions. We could examine the *validity* of the questionnaire in numerous ways; for example, a panel of foremen in an industry could give us the names of workers who were known to be friendly with immigrant workers and the names of those who had shown hostility to immigrants at work. The questionnaire would be valid to the extent that the friendly and the hostile subgroups could be easily distinguished by total scores based on responses to all questions. We could also assess the value of each question by certain technical procedures so that we could eliminate redundant questions. When acceptable limits of reliability, validity, and effectiveness have been met, the questionnaire becomes a useful research tool.

A broad range of attitudes was revealed when a scale of this sort was used to study attitudes towards immigrants in a Canadian community.[7] The topic is relevant to Canadians since one person in eight is a postwar immigrant. The study revealed that long-established Canadians with favorable attitudes towards immigrants were economically well off; they could more easily regulate the contacts they would have with immigrants in contrast to poorer people who were in constant contact and competition with newcomers to the community. Thus, the community's elite were able to show charity and see the value of immigrants to the nation as a whole, whereas the working class had more immediate and personal concerns about immigrants as competitors.

Richard Christie and Florence Geis have opened up one of the most exciting new topics in our field by developing questionnaires to measure a more complex attitude—Machiavellianism.[8] Machiavellianism is the tendency to manipulate and enjoy manipulating other people. Christie and Geis have shown, as Machiavelli had shown in his sixteenth century writings, that there are at least three components of Machiavellianism: a view that other people are generally cowardly and weak, an inclination to use guile and deception in interpersonal contacts, and a general disregard for conventional morality. Each facet is reflected in carefully selected questionnaire items that have been tested for their discriminatory power. For example, the item "Barnum was right when he said there's a sucker born every minute" represents the first facet; "It's wise to flatter important people" reflects the second facet; and "People suffering from incurable diseases should have the choice of

[7] W. E. Lambert, "What Are They Like, These Canadians?" *Canadian Psychologist* 11 (1970): 334–66.

[8] R. Christie and F. Geis, *Studies in Machiavellianism* (New York: Academic Press, 1970).

being put painlessly to death" represents the third facet. The research procedure provides subjects with a means of expressing the intensity of their agreement or disagreement with each item. Furthermore, Christie and Geis developed an ingenious method of measuring Machiavellian tendencies in a subtle way with forced-choice form on the "Mach" scale that allows a subject to think he is hiding his real feelings when he is actually revealing them.[9]

In the next section we will examine how attitudes, such as Machiavellianism, affect behavior. We will also compare questionnaire measures with alternative procedures that rely less on the cooperation of subjects. These alternatives make use of specially created situations that prompt subjects to reveal their private thoughts, feelings, and reaction tendencies without being aware that they are doing so.

The Function of Attitudes

Attitudes play powerful roles in determining our behavior. For example, they affect our judgments and perceptions of others; they influence our speed and efficiency of learning; they help determine the groups we associate with, the professions we finally choose, and even the philosophies we live by. We shall use several research examples here to demonstrate just how attitudes do affect behavior. In the first example, the researchers were more interested in the reactions of groups than in individuals. Instead of measuring each subject's attitudes, the researchers presumed that the majority of the members of the groups studied held stereotyped attitudes that, if the presumption was correct, would influence the behavior of the groups in predictable ways. In the other examples, variations in the type and degree of an individual's attitudes were of prime interest, and measurements of these variations were made by questionnaire techniques.

ATTITUDES AND SOCIAL JUDGMENTS

The first example was carried out in Montreal, a community whose history reveals a French–English schism as socially significant as the North–South schism for Southerners in the United States.[10] The purpose of the study was to determine how French-speaking and English-speaking Montrealers view one another. Since members of both cultural groups

[9] The interested reader can look this up in Christie and Geis, *Studies in Machiavellianism*, chap. 2.
[10] W. E. Lambert, "A Social Psychology of Bilingualism," *Journal of Social Issues* 23 (1967): 91–109.

are identified by the language they speak, the researchers decided to use the spoken language as a means of eliciting stereotyped attitudes. In the first part of the study English-Canadian college students listened to the recorded voices of English and French speakers (all reading versions of the same passage) and indicated on checklists what they thought the personality traits of the speakers might likely be. The students were told that the task was like guessing the characteristics of a person heard on the phone for the first time. They listened to and judged the personalities of ten speakers, some of whom spoke in French. The subjects were told to disregard language and to concentrate on voice and personality in making their ratings. The students were *not* told that in reality they were to hear the voices of five perfectly bilingual speakers, reading once in English and once in Canadian French. The researchers assumed it would be very difficult for Canadians to disregard the language spoken, and any differences in personality assigned to the French and English readers would be likely to stem from the stereotyped attitudes subjects had already developed toward members of the two cultural groups.

As it turned out, the English readers were more favorably evaluated than the French readers. For example, the English-Canadian subjects perceived the English readers as better-looking, taller, more intelligent, more dependable, kinder, more ambitious, and of better character than the French readers. On only one trait were the French readers viewed more favorably—sense of humor.

In the second part of the study, French-Canadian college students went through the same procedure. What is striking is that they, too, evaluated the *English* readers significantly *more* favorably than the French ones on good looks, height, leadership, intelligence, self-confidence, dependability, ambition, sociability, character, and likeableness. This result indicates that many young French-Canadians regard their cultural group as an inferior one. Inferiority of this sort is, in fact, often expressed by bilingual Canadians who sense they are better received by both ethnic groups when speaking English. When they use English they feel more important, as though they were considered more valuable by their social audiences.

The reactions of the French-Canadian students, then, demonstrate that the attitudes of members of a minority group are affected by contacts with groups that are perceived to have higher social status. This tendency has been noted by other researchers in quite different social settings. For example, in communities where they are viewed as inferior by the majority groups, Jews adopt anti-Semitic beliefs and black people take on anti-black attitudes. To better their status or enhance their sense of worth, members of minority groups apparently identify with and unwittingly internalize the stereotyped or prejudiced attitudes of those with power.

Cultural as well as linguistic changes usually take place along sensitive lines of inferiority. Since 1958, when the Montreal study just described was carried out, a contemporary French-Canadian civil rights movement has taken place—similar in many regards to the liberation movements of the black, Chicano, and Indian people in the United States —culminating, in 1970, with a separatist group of French-Canadians turning to kidnapping and violence. Less extreme political leaders are now demanding a separate status for the province of Quebec and for equal political and occupational rights for French Canadians in federal institutions. Apparently the sense of inferiority had become intolerable. One can anticipate that linguistic changes will also follow. At present there is a strong move to "improve" Canadian French along with a smaller countermove to increase pride in the distinctiveness of the French-Canadian language. These inferiority feelings, however, are apparently highly resistant to change. More recent studies show no appreciable shift in the self-image of French Canadians.[11]

ATTITUDES AND LEARNING

If you were asked to learn a series of arguments supporting a point of view that you didn't believe in, would your attitudes get in the way and make it difficult for you to assimilate the new ideas? This question was put to test and the answer, it turns out, is more complex than one might at first think.[12] The topic was segregation. Two groups of white Southern college students were selected to be subjects: one clearly pro-segregation, the other antisegregation in attitudes as measured by a specially devised questionnaire. Both groups were asked to learn thoroughly eleven brief statements arguing against segregation, such as, "The issue of Negro-white integrated education has nothing to do with racial intermarriage," or "The Negro points up the greatest disparity between the theory and our practice of democracy." Each subject read the eleven statements aloud, and then tried to recall as many as possible. Subjects

11 A. d'Anglejan and G. R. Tucker, "Sociolinguistic Correlates of Speech Style in Quebec," in *Social and Ethnic Diversity in the American Speech Community*, ed. R. W. Shuy (Washington, D.C.: Georgetown University Press, 1972); T. LeClerc, "Français académique et Franco-Québécois: Evaluation de ces deux codes linguistiques par les adolescents Canadiens français," (Unpublished M.A. thesis, Institut de Psychologie, Université de Montréal, 1971).

12 E. E. Jones and J. Aneshansel, "The Learning and Utilization of Contravaluent Material," *Journal of Abnormal and Social Psychology* 53 (January 1956): 27–33; E. E. Jones and R. Kohler, "The Effects of Plausibility on the Learning of Controversial Statements," Journal of Abnormal and Social Psychology 57 (May 1958): 315–20.

went through this procedure five times and efficiency of recall was determined for each trial. Those favoring segregation were asked to learn arguments that were *contravaluent,* that is, opposite to their own point of view; the antisegregationists were learning material congruent with their attitudes.

The results of the experiment were clear. Students who were against segregation learned the antisegregation arguments more efficiently than did those who favored segregation. In other words, material congenial with existing attitudes was more readily assimilated. Apparently, the attitudes functioned as a filter, letting congenial ideas enter into memory easily, but stopping or distorting uncongenial ideas.

Suppose the students had been informed that they were to make further use of these arguments—for example, to use them as a rebuttal in a debate. Would the students still learn the congenial arguments better? To test this notion, two more groups of students, one prosegregation and one antisegregation, were told in advance that they were to use the statements later to counter *prosegregation* statements that would be presented to them. In this case it was found that prosegregationists learned the antisegregation arguments *more* efficiently than did the antisegregationists. In other words, prosegregation students apparently became particularly attentive to the antisegregation arguments because it was necessary to know these contravaluent ideas to use them in the rebuttal to follow. The antisegregation arguments apparently passed too easily through the filtering systems of the antisegregationists who had overconfidently assumed that they thoroughly understood such ideas.

In an extension of this experiment, Jones and Kohler wondered whether attitudes would affect the efficiency of learning in the same way if the arguments to be learned were congenial but not logically convincing. As before, they selected students with attitudes pro- or antisegregation and asked them to learn twelve statements, six prosegregation and six antisegregation. Within each group of six, there were three implausible statements based on illogical premises ("if Negroes and whites were meant to live together, they never would have been separated at the beginning of history"), and three plausible statements ("Southerners will have to pay the price of lowered scholastic standards if they yield to the pressures to integrate their schools"). The results demonstrated very convincingly that both groups of students learned better those statements that were congruent with their attitudes *if* they were plausible. But, they learned the *contravaluent* statements better when they were implausible. These findings indicate that people protect their values and attitudes by bulwarking them with good supportive arguments and by enhancing the unreasonableness of the opposing points of view.

These are well designed studies, conducted by first-rate scholars. We can use these studies to point out an important mystery associated with research, especially socially relevant research: Why is is that certain studies are difficult to replicate when thoroughly honest attempts are made to recreate the same phenomena in near-perfect detail? Failures to replicate are important because they recruit other research teams to reexamine the data, thereby forcing resolutions of the conflicting outcomes. And this is one way knowledge advances.

In this case, the Jones and Kohler work was rerun by two separate research teams and both failed to confirm the original results.[13] In fact, Greenwald and Sakamura found that attitudes towards or against American involvement in Vietnam did not affect subjects' learning of propagandist statements about the involvement. More recent research, however, provides strong support for the original results and helps clarify which features of the research plan are essential for the expected outcome.[14] Still, the issue is not finally settled.

Other types of evidence also show that attitudes play a determining role in learning. For example, Albert and Bernice Lott have recently demonstrated that attitudes affect speed and efficiency of associative learning.[15] The work of Kanungo and Dutta on the same topic is especially interesting.[16] Working in India, they found that Bengalis, known to have a strong group identification and pride, had much more difficulty learning a list of unfavorable adjectives attributed to their own group than when the same adjectives were ascribed to some other ethnic group. The Bengalis, however, had very little difficulty learning a list of favorable adjectives that were ascribed to their own group.

Learning a foreign language also seems to depend on the learner's attitudes towards the people who use that language, and on his motives for studying it.[17] With favorable attitudes toward the other group and an

---

13 P. Waley and S. W. Cook, "Attitude as a Determinant of Learning and Memory: A Failure to Conform," *Journal of Personality and Social Psychology* 4 (September 1966): 280–88; A. G. Greenwald and J. S. Sakamura, "Attitude and Selective Learning: Where are the Phenomena of Yesteryear?" *Journal of Personality and Social Psychology* 7 (December 1967): 387–97.

14 A. Lowin, "Further Evidence for an Approach-Avoidance Interpretation of Selective Exposure," *Journal of Experimental and Social Psychology* 5 (July 1969): 265–71; R. Malpass, "Effects of Attitude on Learning and Memory: The Influence of Instruction-Induced Sets," *Journal of Experimental and Social Psychology* 5 (October 1969): 441–53.

15 A. J. Lott, B. E. Lott, and M. L. Walsh, "Learning of Paired Associates Relevant to Differentially Liked Persons," *Journal of Personality and Social Psychology* 16 (October 1970): 274–83.

16 S. Dutta, R. N. Kanungo, and V. Freibergs, "Retention of Affective Material: Effects of Intensity of Affect on Retrieval," *Journal of Personality and Social Psychology* 23 (July 1972).

17 W. E. Lambert and R. C. Gardner, *Attitudes and Motivation in Second Language Learning* (Rowley, Mass.: Newbury House, 1972).

"integrative" motive for studying their language (e.g., seriously wanting to learn about these people and their culture), a learner is more likely to be successful, regardless of his talent for languages, than if his attitude is suspicious or unfriendly and his motives "instrumental" (e.g., needing the language to conduct business with the other group).

ATTITUDES AND BARGAINING SKILL

How does a Machiavellian attitude affect behavior? The portrait of the Machiavellian person has recently been filled in with a good deal of detail. The major features are a coolness and an affective detachment in social settings. The "high Mach" (person who scores high on the Machiavellianism scales) sets his own goals, and then maneuvers people or situations according to his aims. His coolness is shown by his ability to look an accuser straight in the eye while denying any misbehavior. His skill in maneuvering others shows itself in the schemes he can invent to pester and distract them if the situation calls for it. And he obviously enjoys playing with others in this way. He doesn't reveal these traits, though, if the situation is highly structured. Instead, it is in the freer face-to-face social settings where no clear norms hold—permitting him to play his game without rules—that he excels. By contrasting high and low Machs in various contrived situations, Christie and Geis have come to see that the Machiavellian attitude is based on disregard for and a depersonalization of other people. Although the low Mach, through empathy and sensitivity, gets caught up with the feelings of others, the high Mach stays cool and manipulates.

There are also generation-to-generation differences in the degree of Machiavellianism. Manipulating others, it appears, is becoming a more accepted way of thinking and behaving among the younger people in our society. Perhaps this is a natural side-effect of our technological value system. Whether we want to adjust to the trend or react against it, however, we need to understand the attitudinal basis of the phenomenon and its origins. To that end, let us examine one characteristic—the out-maneuvering skill of the Machiavellian—in some detail.

Three college men are called together to take part in an experiment, and are told "You will have a chance to make some money if you are good at bargaining. Ten one-dollar bills will be placed on the table in front of the three of you. . . . The game is over when any two players have made an agreement that the third player cannot get them to break. The money belongs to the two who have made the agreement, and will be divided between them." The men were chosen in advance because they had a high, medium, or low score on the Mach scales. The procedure was repeated for a large number of three-man teams.

Not only do the high Machs win more games (no high Mach failed to be part of a winning pair), but they also make considerably more money, averaging $5.50, $3.15 and $1.30 for the highs, mediums, and lows, respectively. Highs won by maintaining control over the interaction of the triad. It was their cool, impersonal attitude that helped them decide which of the other two could be easily out-bargained and manipulated.

Dorothea Braginsky has traced Machiavellianism back through childhood.[18] She revised and reworded the Mach items to form a "Kiddie Mach" scale for the ten- to twelve-year-old subjects in her experiment. She introduced herself to each child as a home economist working for a cracker company; she was interested in children's opinions about a new "health" cracker (actually plain crackers saturated with quinine). Each child ate a cracker (and then got water and candy to erase the taste), and gave his opinion. Then he was asked to convince another child (chosen to be a middle Mach) to eat as many health crackers as possible so that the lady would get opinions of children who had eaten lots of them. Each child was promised a nickel for every cracker he could get another child to eat!

By now readers should know the outcome of this experiment. The high scorers on the Kiddie Mach scale talked the other children into eating an average of six and a half crackers compared to the only two and three-quarter crackers for low scorers. Although high Mach girls were as effective as high Mach boys in this form of persuasion, they used different tactics. High Mach boys characteristically *distorted* information in their attempts at persuasion, whereas high Mach girls *withheld* information.

ATTITUDES AND PERSONALITY

One might get the impression from the research examples just presented that attitudes are distinct and isolated phenomena. Actually, when one surveys a number of different attitudes simultaneously, it becomes evident that they are interrelated and fall into patterns. In other words, *networks* of attitudes emerge that give form and structure to personalities. We have had glimpses of these patterns of attitudes in the previous research illustrations. For instance, we would anticipate that white Southern college students who are against segregation would likely be sympathetic towards various minority groups. We assume, in other words, that tolerance and prejudice are learned ways of reacting to people in general, not only to specific groups. Generalized ways of

---

[18] Christie and Geis, *Studies in Machiavellianism*, chap. 16.

reacting to people are what we refer to as *personality traits*, and many social psychologists wonder if, in fact, there is anything more to personality traits than distinctive patterns of attitudes.

The possibility that attitudes are basic features of personality was explored by Anisfeld and colleagues in a study of the attitude networks of Jewish high school students.[19] These investigators measured the students' attitudes toward Jews and Gentiles with specially devised anti-Semitism and anti-*goyim* scales. It turned out that attitudes towards Jews and Gentiles were highly correlated, meaning that those students who were most tolerant of Gentiles were also most tolerant of Jews (their own ethnic group), and that those who disliked one group generally disliked the other. Each student was also examined for his general tendencies to be hostile as well as his attitudes toward himself and his parents. Distinct patterns emerged: students with marked hostility tendencies held unfavorable attitudes toward their parents, toward members of the majority group, and toward members of their own ethnic group. In contrast, those with favorable attitudes toward both religious groups also had favorable attitudes toward self and parents. In other words, they had friendly and tolerant personality dispositions.

In one of the most comprehensive studies ever undertaken of the interrelationships of attitudes, it was found that prejudiced attitudes pattern themselves in a rather dramatic fashion.[20] Ethnocentrism, attitudes towards blacks and Jews, patriotism, and political conservation all correlated, presenting the picture of the prejudiced person as anti-Jewish, anti-Negro, antiforeigners, overly and uncritically patriotic, and extremely conservative in political outlook. Adorno and his colleagues also traced these contrasting attitudes back to early family experiences. He found that a person with strong prejudices usually had a highly authoritarian father with a rigid set of expectations.

Certainly more research on the authoritarian personality is needed. Still the studies now available are nevertheless impressive for the emergence of general personality dispositions composed of patterns of attitudes. For example, there seems to be a sharp contrast between people with an open friendliness towards others and those with a reserved negativeness, and between people who adopt a democratic life-style and those with an antidemocratic outlook. Future research will undoubtedly discover deeper attitudes and further explain their development. Even now, however, the evidence is clear that the attitudes we develop

[19] M. Anisfeld et al., "The Structure and Dynamics of the Ethnic Attitudes of Jewish Adolescents," *Journal of Abnormal and Social Psychology* 66 (1963): 31–36.

[20] T. W. Adorno et al., *The Authoritarian Personality* (New York: Harper & Row, 1950).

form consistent patterns and that these attitude networks contribute to the structure of our personalities.[21]

The Development of Attitudes

In our definition of attitudes we emphasized that they are organized, consistent, and habitual ways of thinking, feeling, and reacting to events and persons. We used these adjectives to indicate that attitudes are learned modes of adjustment or, in other words, complex habits. Their development, therefore, should follow standard principles of learning. Our purpose in this section is to introduce three interrelated principles that help explain how attitudes are learned: *association, transfer,* and *need satisfaction.*

Much evidence suggests that we learn feelings and reaction tendencies through association and need satisfaction. That is, we learn to fear and avoid people who are associated with unpleasant happenings and to like and approach those associated with pleasurable happenings. By avoiding unpleasant situations and approaching pleasant situations, we satisfy primary needs for pleasure or comfort. For example, our most basic attitudes are learned in infancy through interaction with our parents. Typically, an infant develops strong favorable attitudes towards parents because they minister to his needs and comfort him. Their presence becomes associated with an infant's contentment and general well-being. In time, as parents become associated with punishment as well as pleasure, the child's attitudes toward them will become complex and ambivalent.

An interesting series of experiments with grade-school children demonstrates how attitudes towards others are learned through association and through need satisfaction.[22] The idea being tested was that a child develops positive attitudes toward others if, while in their presence, he is pleasantly surprised. It should be noted that none of the children chosen for the experiment were close friends at the start of the study. The children were organized in groups of three, and each group was given an interesting game to play. During the games, children in some groups received toys as prizes; other groups received none. Some time later the classroom teacher asked each child to name two others with whom he would like to spend a holiday. It turned out that those who

21 For a current integration of this research, see Triandis, *Attitude and Attitude Change,* chap. 5.

22 B. E. Lott and A. J. Lott, "The Formation of Positive Attitudes Toward Group Members," *Journal of Abnormal and Social Psychology* 61 (September 1960): 297–300.

had received prizes chose more of their play-group associates as holiday friends than did those who got no toys. As predicted, positive attitudes developed when play-group members were associated with a
pleasurable event. In recent follow-up research, the same investigators
found that very favorable attitudes are formed when the rewards are
delivered immediately rather than promised and only later delivered.[23]

These findings lend support to the principles underlying the research,
and help explain how unfavorable attitudes can develop, or become intensified, in social contexts where we experience disappointments or
failures in the presence of members of some distinctive group. A person's disappointments in school or at work, for example, can become
associated with the presence of certain others who, by comparison, are
more successful. In such instances, unfavorable attitudes are revealed
in such remarks as "How can you get ahead with so many of *them*
around!" By an individual's placing the blame for his difficulties on
others, he artificially enhances his self-respect. In a similar fashion, positive attitudes towards members of the "old gang" with whom we have
had our good times are likely to persist or become more positive. Extending the same principles, we find that members of a whole community
often develop negative attitudes towards racial or immigrant groups
whom they associate with their economic difficulties.

Although we develop feelings and reaction tendencies toward others
through association and need satisfaction, we acquire thoughts and beliefs in a different fashion. In the early stages of their development, in
fact, attitudes learned by association and need satisfaction are often
characterized by the learner's inability to comprehend *why* he feels and
reacts as he does. This inability to comprehend makes him especially
attentive to other people's expressions of thoughts and beliefs, and he
may readily adopt these as a means of justifying his own feelings and
reaction tendencies. Our purpose here is to introduce the principle of
transfer, which helps explain how we learn the thought-belief components of attitudes from other people.

Apparently we learn attitudes through transfer essentially the same
way we learn meanings of concepts through instruction. Thus, a child
will immediately develop a meaning for *zebra* when told it is a horse-
like animal with up-and-down stripes. Here two unrelated ideas ("horse"
and "up-and-down stripes") are brought into a novel but meaningful
combination for the first time. In a similar fashion, people can transfer attitudes to one another by suggesting ways to reorganize and integrate certain basic ideas. In a close relationship, feelings and reaction

[23] A. J. Lott et al., "Liking for Persons as a Function of Incentive and Drive
During Acquisition," *Journal of Personality and Social Psychology* 14 (January
1970): 66–76.

tendencies can also be transferred as well as thoughts and beliefs. For instance, someone could transfer a completely favorable attitude towards immigrants by describing them as "maltreated," "hardworking," "friendly," and "lively." Or he could transfer a negative attitude by describing them as "foreign," "undependable," "dirty," and "untrustworthy."

Although attitudes are very commonly learned through transfer, we are not often fully aware of the principle's significance until we encounter such situations as the following: In a midwestern American community that had no Jewish or Negro residents at all, anti-Semitism and prejudice toward Negroes were found to be as strong and prevalent among teenagers as in large eastern cities heavily populated by Jews and Negroes.[24] In this case, the unfavorable attitudes could not have been learned through association; they must have been transferred.

Of course we don't incorporate all attitudes directed toward us. That we are selective about which attitudes we pick up means that need satisfaction is usually involved when attitudes are transferred. As children, we pay attention to and usually adopt the attitudes of our parents. We do so because being like them assures us of their affection at the same time we strengthen our feeling of belonging in the family. Children's needs for affection and belonging are not always satisfied in the family, of course; children often show their hostility by failing to accept the transfer of their parents' attitudes, or by adopting contrary ones.

We also adopt attitudes of other important people outside the family. As we grow older, we incorporate attitudes that seem appropriate for belonging to groups we consider important. Sometimes we change attitudes as a means of leaving one group and becoming part of another. A classic study by Newcomb demonstrates how the need-satisfaction principle works in determining attitude transfer.[25] Newcomb made repeated examinations over a four-year period of the attitudes and personalities of students in a small New England women's college. Most students came from politically and socially conservative homes, but the college faculty and the advanced students had created a decidedly liberal political atmosphere on campus. A majority of the girls adopted the liberal values of the community, but a minority showed no change, some even intensifying their conservatism. By the fourth year it was evident that those who had become liberal had done so both in order to obtain approval of students and faculty and to satisfy their urge to

[24] J. F. Rosenblith, "A Replication of 'Some Roots of Prejudice,'" *Journal of Abnormal and Social Psychology* 44 (1949): 470–89.

[25] T. M. Newcomb, *Personality and Social Change: Attitude Formation in a Student Community* (New York: Holt, Rinehart & Winston, 1943).

become independent of their parents. In contrast, those who remained conservative, apparently because of their timidity and feelings of inadequacy, had become psychologically withdrawn from the community and were thereby immune from influence. As a group, they kept their original attitudes, either to protect themselves from a threatening social environment or to maintain the affection of their parents. Thus, important social needs were satisfied for both those who adopted and those who failed to adopt new attitudes.

There is one further aspect to attitude development, namely, when and how do children distinguish between members of their own group and members of different groups? Lambert and Klineberg recently conducted a large-scale cross-national study to explore children's views of their own group and of foreign peoples.[26] Over 3000 children—six-, ten-, and fourteen-year-olds from ten nations in the world—were interviewed and asked a standard set of questions:

What are you?

What else are you?

Tell me which people in foreign lands are like us? Which are not like us?

Tell me why you say they are similar or different?

What else do you know about (each of) these people?

Where did you learn about them?

Tell me about us—what are we (own ethnic group) like?

Suppose you hadn't been born where you were, what nation would you most like to live in? Which least?

This research revealed that, long before they reach school age, children are intrigued by the distinctions between in-groups and out-groups that society forces on them, and this is so as much for Bantu children in South Africa as it is for Israeli, Lebanese, Brazilian, Japanese, Canadian, or American youngsters. Children apparently learn what in-groups and out-groups are through *contrasts* drawn for them by parents or other family members. The Bantu child learns what it is to be a Bantu by having Bantus contrasted with people who are not Bantu. In this way a basic in-group–out-group schema is apparently activated in the child's thinking, and this mental structure very likely stays with him for life.[27]

---

[26] W. E. Lambert and O. Klineberg, *Children's Views of Foreign Peoples* (New York: Appleton-Century-Crofts, 1967). A briefer report of the same work can be found in Lambert and Klineberg, "The Development of Children's Views of Foreign Peoples," *Childhood Education* 45 (January 1969): 247–53.

[27] H. R. Isaacs, *Scratches on Our Minds* (New York: John Day, 1958).

The ways in which parents and others deal with the child's early questions are crucial. They can take the most expedient route (and most parents in the survey seemed to do so) and draw the distinction too sharply and too emotionally. For example, they may caricature the other group: "Oh, *they* beat their children," "They drink too much," "They are lazy," "Their hair is long and dirty," or "They like to live in slums." The child soon gets the idea that his group is superior. Lambert and Klineberg find that this training through contrasts starts the whole process of stereotyping people—foreign peoples as well as one's own group. Because attitudes once formed are so resistant to change, we see in this example how delicate the process of attitude formation really is.

The Modification of Attitudes

At first glance, the changing of attitudes might seem to be a simple matter. Since attitudes are learned, it should be easy enough to modify their intensity or replace an undesirable one. Attitudes, however, are not as easily modified or replaced as they are learned. As we have seen, once an attitude is developed, it becomes an integral aspect of an individual's personality, affecting his whole style of behavior. Changing one attitude is not easy because it becomes part of a network that gives order to one's personality. Well-planned attempts to modify attitudes often only succeed in altering the thought-belief component without modifying feelings and reaction tendencies so that in time the attitude may easily revert to its former state. Those attitudes developed in the home or through early experiences in groups are particularly instrumental in forming the structure of attitude networks, and are especially resistant to modification. For instance, we might expect French-speaking Canadians to have rejected a sense of inferiority over the past fifteen years, but, as already mentioned, this has not happened yet. Similarly, we might think that the attitudes and values of American college students would have changed since 1950. Charles Morris and Linwood Small recently surveyed attitudes and were surprised that students' conceptions have changed little over the twenty-year period. Students still define "the good life" in approximately the same way and by roughly equivalent percentages as students did in 1950.[28]

Nevertheless, we know that attitudes can be changed under certain

[28] C. Morris and L. Small, "Changes in Conceptions of the Good Life by American College Students from 1950 to 1970," *Journal of Personality and Social Psychology* 20 (November 1970): 254–60.

conditions. Some of the college girls we just talked about in Newcomb's study demonstrably shifted from conservative to liberal attitudes in the process of leaving home and becoming part of a new community. Far more research is needed to explain both the persistence and the modifiability of attitudes. Although no final answers are available, we have certain guidelines. Attitudes are particularly resistant to change—

a) if they have been learned early in life

b) if they have been learned by association as well as transfer

c) if they help satisfy needs

d) if they have been deeply integrated into one's personality and style of behaving.

LEARNING AND ATTITUDE CHANGE

Social psychologists are guided by such general rules in their attempts to change attitudes. They realize that if attitudes are to be replaced or their intensity modified, the alternatives must be presented very tactfully. If habitual modes of feeling and reacting are to be altered, actual social settings, or contrived experimental ones, must be so arranged that new ways of responding can be learned. The techniques used must facilitate replacement and learning.

It is our view that to change or replace an attitude, one must work with the principles of transfer, association, and need satisfaction. Many psychologists are engaged in research to determine what approaches, if any, are effective in changing attitudes through *transfer*. The findings to date suggest that new attitudes are more likely to be transferred through face-to-face contacts and group discussions than through impersonal lectures or mass media communications.[29] But the personalities of those making the contacts can limit their effectiveness as agents of transfer. One would expect that attitudes are most easily transferred when the learner is able to identify with his social "teachers" and desires to be like them, as in the case of the child and his parents. But the research on this issue is not that clear. Some investigations suggest that the more trustworthy and attractive the influencer is, the more likely his message will get through and affect existing attitudes;[30] other studies show that there is no simple relationship between the likeability

[29] For a review of these studies, see D. Krech, R. S. Crutchfield, and E. L. Ballachey, *Individual in Society* (New York: McGraw-Hill, 1962), chap. 7.

[30] See J. Mills and J. Harvey, "Opinion Change as a Function of When Information About the Communicator is Received and Whether He is Attractive or Expert," *Journal of Personality and Social Psychology* 21 (January 1972): 52–55; also see D. Kretch et al., *Individual in Society*.

of the influencer and his success as an agent of change.[31] For example, in certain studies it is the *disliked* rather than the liked person who is more effective in changing attitudes. In other cases it is the stranger who is more effective than a friend in changing someone's attitudes.

Extensive use is also made of the principle of *need satisfaction* in attempts to alter attitudes. If a person realizes that it is to his advantage to change, he will be encouraged to learn to change. For example, the new ideas incorporated in a persuasive message can be presented with the endorsement of group leaders or people of high social standing. If those who receive the message realize that being accepted by others depends on their adopting a different set of attitudes, they will try to change their attitudes. If they are given opportunities to reorganize their beliefs and their personal needs, the likelihood that they will change is also improved. Zimbardo and Ebbesen, for example, argue that *active participation* by the target person (as in role playing) is more effective in reorganizing beliefs and needs than is simple exposure to persuasive communications.[32]

A change of attitudes may also take place if appropriate conditions are provided to learn new ways of feeling and reacting through *association*. Prejudiced attitudes have been changed in integrated housing projects and military camps. In these instances, blacks and whites live together as social equals and demonstrate to each other that their behavior is not as different as many may have previously believed. Feelings and reaction tendencies can also be modified, at least superficially, by movies or TV productions that favorably portray the everyday life and experiences of members of minority groups so that a viewer may identify with the main characters. The balance here is delicate, however. If a person experiences personal failures or disappointments, he may, through association, use a minority group's misery and squalor as a source of personal hope, convincing himself that at least he's still better off.

PERSONALITY AND ATTITUDE CHANGE

Although extensive research is continuing on methods of ordering and presenting persuasive communications or creating social contexts for learning new attitudes, other research teams are directing attention to the personality characteristics of those whose attitudes are to be

31 W. McGuire, "The Nature of Attitudes and Attitude Change," in *The Handbook of Social Psychology*, ed. G. Lindzey and E. Aronson (Reading, Mass.: Addison-Wesley, 1969), vol. 3, chap. 21.

32 P. Zimbardo and E. B. Ebbesen, *Influencing Attitudes and Changing Behavior* (Reading, Mass.: Addison-Wesley, 1969); see also H. Triandis, *Attitudes and Attitude Change*.

changed. Because attitudes are tenaciously linked with personality, any attempts to change attitudes will be limited until more is understood about the relation of attitudes to personality. The work of Hovland and his associates at Yale and that of Festinger and his colleagues have already advanced our understanding of this problem.[33]

The Yale group has sketched out some of the personality characteristics that distinguish the persuasible from the nonpersuasible person.[34] Few people have the ideal quality of *discriminating flexibility*; that is, few people are able to recognize new ideas directed at them while being able to distinguish and reject what is irrelevant. Most people deviate from this ideal toward extremes. The gullible person is characterized by a marked dependence on other people and a lack of ability to critically evaluate others' propositions. This combination of traits makes him especially prone to adopt other people's beliefs or any propositions that are authoritatively presented. At the other extreme is the person highly resistant to persuasion; he appears to lack an ability to comprehend the ideas communicated to him. He is usually negative to authority, rigid and obtuse in his thinking, and voluntarily inattentive to new ideas.

Recent evidence suggests that there is a reliable sex difference in persuasibility, women being more persuasible than men. Some have argued that this is simply an example of the female trait of yielding, while others are of the opinion that women are more attentive to spoken or written communications and also better at comprehending verbal material.[35]

This line of investigation has been extended by McGuire in his studies of the strategies people sometimes develop to "immunize" themselves against persuasion by building up a resistance against other people's beliefs or attitudes.[36] Apparently a person can enhance his ability to be critical of persuasive information by strengthening his commitments to his own beliefs, or by anchoring his beliefs in broader attitudinal networks.[37]

Milton Rosenberg has probed very deeply into personality to examine

---

[33] L. Festinger, *A Theory of Cognitive Dissonance* (New York: Harper & Row, 1957).

[34] I. L. Janis et al., *Personality and Persuasibility* (New Haven, Conn.: Yale University Press, 1959).

[35] W. J. McGuire, "The Nature of Attitudes and Attitude Change."

[36] W. J. McGuire, "Persistence of the Resistance to Persuasion Induced by Various Types of Prior Belief Defenses," *Journal of Abnormal and Social Psychology* 64 (1962): 241–48.

[37] McGuire, "The Nature of Attitude and Attitude Change." For a technical discussion of the relation of personality to persuasibility, see also W. J. McGuire, "Personality and Susceptibility to Social Influence," in *Handbook of Personality Theory and Research*, ed. E. Borgatta and W. W. Lambert (Chicago: Rand McNally, 1968), chap. 24.

attitude change.[38] He wondered whether an established system of attitude components could be broken up, and then, whether the system would reorganize itself if one component were experimentally changed. For example, what effect would a drastic change of a feeling component have on the thought-belief and reaction tendency components of an attitude? His technique was to place subjects under deep hypnosis and tamper with their feelings toward certain emotional issues. To those with strong anti-black attitudes, he suggested that, after awakening, they would be "very much in favor of blacks moving into white neighborhoods. The mere idea of blacks moving into white neighborhoods will give you a happy, exhilarated feeling." To others who favored American aid to foreign countries, he suggested that "the mere idea of the United States giving economic aid to foreign nations will disgust and displease you." He also told subjects that they would be unable to remember where the planted idea had come from until they were given a certain signal at some later time. Only then would they recall that the hypnotist had given them the idea, and they would revert to their original feelings. All subjects were brought out of the hypnotic state, but some were kept under the influence of the suggested change for as long as a week before the signal was finally given them.

The reactions of the subjects to these planted feelings are revealing. Thoughts, beliefs, and reaction tendencies changed so as to be consistent with the new feelings. During the one-week waiting period there were signs of reorganization of whole networks of related attitudes; and even after the original feelings were restored, the new attitude organizations persisted to some degree, or at least the intensity of the original attitudes was reduced.

THE DESIRE FOR CONSISTENCY
AND ATTITUDE CHANGE

A number of social psychologists are currently exploring the tendency of people to keep their attitudes logically consistent. This interest stems from the ideas of Fritz Heider who was convinced that people seek balanced, harmonious relations among their attitudes and behaviors, and are psychologically upset until a state of balance is achieved.[39] When the significance of this idea sunk in, some of the most promising theories of attitude change began to appear. First, Osgood and Tannenbaum

[38] M. Rosenberg, C. I. Hovland, W. J. McGuire, R. P. Abelson, and J. W. Brehm, *Attitude Organization and Change* (New Haven, Conn.: Yale University Press, 1960), chap. 2; see also G. Edwards, "Duration of Post-Hypnotic Effect," *British Journal of Psychiatry* 109, whole no. 459 (1963): 259–66; and M. T. Orne, "The Nature of the Hypnotic Phenomenon: Recent Empirical Studies," *American Psychologist* 18 (July 1963): 431.

[39] F. Heider, *The Psychology of Interpersonal Relations* (New York: John Wiley, 1958).

showed that people will alter their attitudes when incongruities become obvious.[40] For example, consider the recent visit of President Nixon to China. The Chinese people, we will assume, had a highly favorable attitude toward Chairman Mao and a somewhat suspicious and negative attitude toward President Nixon. But once they saw photos of a smiling Mao tête-à-tête with Nixon, their enthusiasm increased and, presumably, the underlying attitude toward Nixon became more favorable. Note that there is no direct transfer of attitude components involved here. Rather, people are left to reorganize the relationship between Nixon and Mao and modify *their own* attitudes so as to achieve a logical consistency among them.

Festinger and his colleagues have taken this basic idea several steps further.[41] They argue that people have strong internal tendencies to resolve inconsistencies between their attitudes and their behavior. A person who smokes may have trouble reconciling this activity with his knowledge that smoking can be unhealthy, just as a person who buys a Pontiac may have trouble with his recollection that the Fords he test-drove were equally attractive. Festinger's research has shown that people develop strategies to rid themselves of presumably powerful, uneasy feelings that accompany such inconsistencies. Goaded by the conflict, the smoker may give up cigarettes and increase the intensity of his attitude toward medical research, or he may keep on smoking and convince himself that medical facts about smoking are of dubious value. The Pontiac owner will likely seek out other owners of Pontiacs for support and, perhaps unconsciously, actively search out cases of Ford owners who have had trouble with their cars.

Currently, researchers are looking further into the psychological events that transpire just after a difficult, irreversible decision has been made. The typical first reaction is regret which dissipates in time as the decision maker conducts an internal debate to devalue the rejected alternative and enhance the value of the choice actually made.[42] This attitude balancing may account for important individual differences in making decisions and staying with them. Some people (presumably those with shorter regret spans) can make decisions and then forget the matter, while others (with longer regret spans) are haunted for a long time. Thus, some people enjoy shopping for anything from Pontiacs to trivia while others hate the whole activity. However, the main point is that

[40] C. E. Osgood and P. H. Tannenbaum, "The Principle of Congruity in the Prediction of Attitude Change," *Psychological Review* 62 (January 1955): 42–55.

[41] Festinger, *A Theory of Cognitive Dissonance.*

[42] J. W. Brehm and R. A. Wicklund, "Regret Dissonance Reduction as a Function of Postdecision Salience of Dissonant Information," *Journal of Personality and Social Psychology* 14 (January 1970): 1–7; L. Festinger, *Conflict, Decision, and Dissonance* (Stanford, Calif.: University of Stanford Press, 1964).

these studies open up to research the chain of events preceding and following decisions, so that in time we may develop means of helping people change their own inconsistent, unproductive or simply prejudiced attitudes.

It should be apparent in these examples that a person changes his own attitudes to reduce the inconsistency between them and his behavior. But it has also come to light that when people are pressured into behaving in a manner inconsistent with their attitudes, change is only likely to occur if the pressure is there, but not too strong. For instance, if you were asked to make a public statement in favor of an issue you were really against, you might experience uneasiness about the inconsistency between your ideals and your actions. But if you were very well paid for doing so, you might be less bothered ("Who wouldn't for that price?") than if you were simply talked into making the statement and received little in return for doing so. According to Festinger, the greater the inconsistency between ideals and actions, the stronger the psychological *dissonance* and the more intense the need to reduce the inconsistency. Thus, the person who received no pay for making the statement would be more prone to change his original attitude because there was a great inconsistency between his ideals and his actions.

The power of this notion was demonstrated in an experiment run by Festinger and Carlsmith.[43] Each student spent an hour at a very boring task, and each was asked to tell the next student waiting to undergo the same ordeal that it was enjoyable and rather interesting. Some students were paid one dollar, others twenty dollars for making this false statement. As predicted, those who were paid the smaller amount changed their original attitudes towards the task. By the time they were questioned later, they had apparently convinced themselves that the job really wasn't that bad. For those paid twenty dollars, the task remained just as boring in retrospect, even though they had lied about it; however, they experienced much less uneasiness about their actions since they could argue, "Who wouldn't for twenty dollars?" The one-dollar students were upset about their actions and rationalized their unease. It is of particular interest to us here that attitudes change under these conditions of dissonance, and that those students involved did the changing on their own.

Another important facet to this problem is presented by the work of Daryl Bem.[44] Bem is bothered by the fact that dissonance theory has

[43] L. Festinger and J. M. Carlsmith, "Cognitive Consequences of Forced Compliance," *Journal of Abnormal and Social Psychology* 58 (1959): 203–10.

[44] D. J. Bem, "Self-Perception: An Alternative Interpretation of Cognitive Dissonance Phenomena," *Psychological Review* 74 (1967): 183–200; D. J. Bem and H. J. McConnell, "Testing the Self-Perception Explanation of Dissonance Phenomena: On the Salience of Premanipulation Attitudes," *Journal of Personality and Social Psychology* 14 (January 1970): 23–31.

taken us too far from observable behavior. Concepts such as *dissonance, needs to reduce inconsistencies,* and *regret* refer to private events. If these can be made less mysterious and more open to direct observation, all the better for social psychology, Bem argues. His theory of self-perception is offered as an alternative interpretation of the same pre-decision and postdecision events. He believes that people come to know and categorize their own internal states (attitudes included) by observing *themselves* in action in specified settings. The subject, in other words, becomes his own observer. When information about an internal state is obscure or ambiguous, the person involved is in no better state than an outside observer in trying to infer or interpret his own feelings or attitudes. Thus, if a person were to be paid one dollar for falsifying his beliefs about a monotonous task, he, like anyone else observing him, would infer that his own beliefs are being appropriately expressed, that is, that the task isn't so boring. If any of us were to observe a person telling a little white lie for twenty dollars we would have no basis for inferring anything about the person's true attitudes. Nor would a subject in that experiment have any grounds for assuming that his own attitudes were related to his actions in that instance. For Bem, therefore, the attitude changes attributed to dissonance can be more simply explained as common-sense interpretations of the individual observing himself when he tells a lie. Bem finds no reason to introduce concepts, such as powerful dissonance needs, that force an internal reconciliation of attitudes and actions. We can be certain that much good research will be generated by the heat of this debate between Bem and the true believers of dissonance theory.

In Perspective

In this chapter we have been concerned with attitudes, defined as organized and consistent manners of thinking, feeling, and reacting with regard to people, groups, and social issues. In the process of coping with our social environments we develop attitudes and, once developed, they facilitate our adjustments by regularizing our reactions to recurring events. When attitudes are rigidly organized, however, they constrict the richness of our experiences. Because we tend to categorize people and events too readily into overstructured patterns of thought, our feelings and reactions to experiences become more routinized than personalized.

Social psychologists have put much effort and ingenuity into the invention of methods of measuring attitudes. Because attitudes are not directly observable, they must be inferred either from careful observation of people's behavior in certain permissive social situations or from patterns of responses made on questionnaires specially designed to reflect probable modes of thinking, feeling, and reacting. To be of value, measures of attitudes must meet stringent standards of reliability, validity, and comprehensiveness. But the usefulness of the questionnaire technique is often limited because respondents, even when answering anonymously, become suspicious and misrepresent their thoughts and feelings. Because of this, experimental methods are being devised that permit us to infer attitude components from behavior so that subjects remain unaware that they are revealing cues about their real thoughts, feelings, or reaction tendencies.

Much of our social behavior is influenced by our attitudes. They affect our judgments and perceptions, our efficiency in learning, our reactions to others, and even our basic philosophies of life. Ultimately, the numerous attitudes we develop come to cluster into distinctive patterns and these patterns give our personalities their distinctive styles.

We view attitudes as complex habit systems and as such we expect their development to follow principles of learning much as other types of habit and abilities do. Evidence suggests that we learn two of the elements of attitudes—the feeling and reaction-tendency components—through *association* and *need satisfaction*. That is, we learn to fear and avoid people and events associated with unpleasant happenings and to like and approach events associated with pleasurable happenings. We typically acquire our thoughts and beliefs (the third component) from important people in our social world who *transfer* to us their thoughts and beliefs. Through social communication, we not only receive components of attitudes through transfer, but we also transmit our own belief to others.

Attempts to modify or replace attitudes rely on the same principles of learning. Because it is apparently much more difficult to change or forget attitudes than it is to learn them, we are beginning to appreciate the large and crucial role early socialization plays in attitude development.

Various strategies to modify attitudes are being investigated and compared. One promising new approach emphasizes people's normal desire to be logically consistent in what they think, feel, and do. Researchers have found that when one attitude component is experimentally modified, the other components realign themselves compatibly. There are even signs that people will change their own attitudes, often without being aware of it, when logical inconsistencies in their beliefs and feelings are brought to their attention or when they are given opportunities to observe themselves objectively in interaction with others.

The Psychological Significance of Social Interaction

chapter five

Social Interaction

The focus of this chapter is on the relationships that develop among people when they come into social contact. Within the limits of the information now available, we shall attempt to explain how human associations—friendships, cliques of acquaintances, or small groups—get established, how they typically progress through time, and how those involved are affected by the give and take of the relationship. The discussion will be organized around the concept of social interaction, the process by which people influence one another through the mutual interchange of thoughts, feelings, and reactions. Once we can recognize this process and understand some of the ways it functions, many recurring episodes that fill our daily lives take on a new significance and fascination. We begin to understand, for example, what actually takes place when two people become acquainted and in time become attracted to or dependent on each other, why so many close relationships ultimately dissolve, why friends adjust to each other's ways of behaving, or why members of a group react against someone whose attitudes and values are out of line. We also come to understand ourselves better, since none

photo by Chris Lund

of us is ever really free from some form of social interaction. Even in our moments of solitude, we have others in our thoughts as we search for the meaning of ongoing relationships, or as we review how we acted or should have acted with others, and rehearse how we and they are likely to behave in future situations.

We shall examine two aspects of social interaction here. First we present the learning theorist's approach to social relationships, and describe how the process of interaction gets started, how it develops, and how those involved are affected when they receive or fail to receive satisfaction through associating with each other. Then we look at interaction as a system of reactions involving two or more people, and examine how that system functions. Throughout we will highlight current methods of analyzing the behavior of those interacting—behavior that runs its course so swiftly that most of its finer features pass unnoticed.

Social Interaction and the Principle of Need Satisfaction

Surprisingly enough, young children have a very objective conception of social interaction, one that approaches closely the learning theorist's view of the process. Dorothy Flapan asked six-year-olds to watch and later describe the person-to-person communication displayed in short movies.[1] Their descriptions, in contrast to those of older children, dwelt on overt actions of the characters, the settings of each scene, and the more dramatic events. For them the characters were seen as actors and reactors, and relatively little attention was given to the inferred psychological content of the episodes or the thinking or aspirations of the characters portrayed. As we shall see, adult specialists in person-

[1] D. Flapan, *Children's Understanding of Social Interaction* (New York: Teachers College Press, 1968).

to-person communication share this objective, factual outlook on the process.

From the point of view of the learning theorist, interaction gets underway and is maintained when participants receive *reinforcements* for interacting. That is, when they receive something they need or want through associating with one another. We will follow several examples of how this important principle of learning works in social relationships, starting with the interaction of a pigeon and an experimenter. Then we can appreciate how the same principles of learning apply to the more complex cases of human social relationships.

AN EXPERIMENTER AND A PIGEON
IN INTERACTION

Imagine an experimenter placing a pigeon in a large, rectangular box for the first time in its life. The particular box we have in mind is commonly known as a Skinner Box, after B. F. Skinner of Harvard who, through his ingenious research, has demonstrated the tremendous importance of reinforcements in all forms of behavior.[2] The box is empty except for a coin-sized disc attached to the floor at one end; through an opening in the top, the experimenter can watch the animal's every move. The pigeon has been kept hungry and wants food, while the experimenter wants to control the pigeon's behavior. He wants the pigeon to peck at the disc, not just once, but with a certain regularity, and in line with an experimental plan. The experimenter's interest in his relationship with the pigeon is something more than that of an animal trainer's. His professional interest demands that he be able to control systematically the pigeon's actions. Skinner demonstrates convincingly that the animal's behavior can indeed be controlled, as we shall see, but what is of even greater interest for us at the moment is the fascinating symbolic relationship that develops between the experimenter and pigeon as they interact.

At first, the pigeon moves nervously about the box, exploring, attempting to get out, incidentally pecking here and there. Whenever it moves close to the disc, the experimenter rolls a kernel of corn into the box and the hungry animal eats it up immediately. After receiving reinforcements each time it was close to the disc, the pigeon tends to stay in that area and eventually pecks the disc itself. This is a big event for the experimenter. Although anticipated, it is nevertheless exciting to have molded the animal's behavior to this extent. It turns out to be a

[2] B. F. Skinner, *Science and Human Behavior* (New York: Macmillan, 1953);
B. F. Skinner, *Beyond Freedom and Dignity* (New York: Knopf, 1971).

big event for the pigeon, too, because pecking the disc calls out a small handful of kernels. In a surprisingly short time, the interaction is well underway. The pigeon directs itself to the disc and pecks it with increasing regularity while the experimenter carefully follows the animal's activity and reinforces each peck at the disc. If the experimenter errs or delays in giving corn as the big event approaches, the pigeon may move away and the *shaping* has to start again with the experimenter patiently awaiting the pigeon's return. Thus, the experimenter's corn-giving, considering his own needs and the rules he has set up, is under the control of the pigeon's disc-pecking in the same way that the pigeon's pecking response is controlled by the reinforcements provided by the experimenter. The pigeon seems to have his own rules of the game, and the experimenter's major task is to discover what these are.

The interaction continues as long as each participant receives reinforcements from the other, but it can be stopped or modified in several ways. The pigeon will, in time, satisfy his hunger and terminate the interaction by moving away from the disc, or the experimenter can decide at any moment that he has proven his point and temporarily terminate the association by taking the animal back to its cage. The experimenter can also take the upper hand and *extinguish* the pigeon's disc-pecking by withholding reinforcements, and the pigeon will then gradually stop pecking the disc. Or the experimenter can modify the regularity of reinforcements and require the pigeon to peck at different rates. For example, he can get the animal to peck twenty or more times for one grain of corn if he works up to this ratio gradually. Or he can make speed of pecking a requirement for reward and dole out his reinforcements only for very fast bursts. In such a case, the pigeon will peck the disc at an amazingly fast pace.

The rudimentary form of social interaction apparent in this example, then, gets underway and develops because both participants through association receive reinforcements that satisfy their own particular needs. How well can this basic principle of learning account for more complex forms of interaction?

TWO OF A KIND IN INTERACTION

Consider now the development of a relationship between two pigeons.[3] In this case, the experimenter is more in the background. He also has a different plan in mind—to get the pigeons to work cooperatively. To do so, he first places them on either end of a small table, which is divided in the center by a glass partition. A row of three discs lies on

---

[3] Skinner, *Science and Human Behavior*, chap. 19.

each side of the partition. The buttons are wired in pairs so that if any two opposite discs (one on each side of the glass) are depressed at the same time, a kernel of corn rolls out to each bird. The pigeons have to learn that they will be rewarded only when they peck any pair of buttons simultaneously. Actually pigeons learn this problem with little difficulty, and in doing so, they learn to cooperate. At first, each explores its own compartment and is rewarded for pecking a disc. Slowly the reinforcements are held off until, by chance, both pigeons happen to strike opposite discs simultaneously. When this happens both are immediately and amply reinforced. After two or three repetitions of this sort, each pigeon tends to hover over a disc on its side. Then they peck in unison and are rewarded. On each trial the experimenter selects one particular pair of discs (from the three possible) as the "correct" one, and the birds soon learn to search it out together. Typically, one pigeon takes the lead and the other, watching attentively, follows. (You might want to speculate about the outcome of interaction if two "leaders" or two "followers" were teamed up.)

The same experiment has been carried out with young children.[4] The two youngsters face each other at a table separated in the middle by a glass partition and are told they may play as they like with the materials before them. Among the playthings available to both is a stationary metal plate with three holes and a metal rod. The metal parts have been connected electrically so that if both children happen to stick the rods in corresponding holes simultaneously, their joint action would be automatically reinforced with sweets. Reward chutes would deliver candies to both children if they, like the pigeons, learned to respond in unison.

Although the children were not even given a hint on how to play the game, their coordinated responses increased rapidly once they caught on. With the children as with pigeons, each participant became aware of the other's importance in the sense that neither would be rewarded unless he functioned as a mirror image of the other. The interaction was maintained in both cases because reinforcements were contingent upon the mutual dependence of a follower on a leader and a leader on his partner.

PARENT AND INFANT IN INTERACTION

Infants learn to speak by interacting with others who already know how to speak. Although every normal infant has the genetic potential

[4] N. H. Azrin and O. R. Lindsley, *Journal of Abnormal and Social Psychology* 52 (1956): 100–102.

to learn any language, members of his own linguistic group restrict attention to a particular selection of sounds. Parents differentially reinforce the infant's early babbling by giving him affectionate rewards (in the form of smiles, caresses, even cries of delight) when his utterances come somewhat close to actual words.[5] Through the interaction, the child's need for affectionate attention and the parents' desire to have their child become a communicating member of the family are both satisfied. Because it is mutually satisfying, the interaction continues and the child's further attempts to reproduce appropriate words are reinforced. When the child communicates his desire for a drink of milk with a sound that vaguely resembles "milk," his attentive parents may immediately comply with his request. Signs of the infant's progress in speaking are reinforcements for the parents just as their compliance with his request is a reinforcement for the child. But the compliance not only increases the likelihood that the child will learn to repeat the word, it also strengthens his tendencies to demand other things. That is, the child also learns the instrumental value of verbal interaction—through communication he can get what he wants from others. The parents could, of course, refrain from giving the milk until a near-perfect pronunciation is achieved. By not complying immediately, they would not only increase the child's linguistic exactitude, but also discourage the development of a general tendency to demand. There are two points to note here. Social interaction between parent and child is maintained because both participants receive satisfactions through the relationship; and through interaction, both parties learn basic styles of reacting to others. For example, overattentive parents could make a "demander" of their child and the child, in turn, could make "compliers" of his parents if he showed them affection only when they yielded to his demands. In fact, Christie suggests that it is in this context that little children may learn to be Machiavellian.[6] If the mother is a low Mach, for example, she may be easily manipulated to give reinforcements (through subtle cues, such as little cries, or outright demands) and thereby contribute to the development of the child's skill at manipulating.

THE CASE OF VERBAL REINFORCEMENT

It has been demonstrated repeatedly that a person can manipulate another's conversation with the appropriate use of social reinforcements. For instance, in one investigation, college students were asked to speak

[5] Skinner, *Science and Human Behavior*, chap. 19.

[6] R. Christie and F. L. Geis, *Studies in Machiavellianism* (New York: Academic Press, 1970).

whatever words happened to come to mind.[7] The experimenter led the subjects to believe that he was only interested in the vagaries of their ideas, whereas actually he was trying to direct the form of their verbalizations. He listened attentively and said "good" or "uh-*huh*" whenever a subject said a plural noun. Very shortly, the rate of saying plural nouns was markedly increased, and this, as in the pigeon example, constituted a strong reinforcement for the experimenter. Thus, the verbal reinforcements "good" or "uh-*huh*" oriented the subject's selection of words according to that desired by the experimenter. The subjects may have consciously interpreted "good" to be a form of encouragement to select and then continue in a certain mode of communication in much the same way as most people select and change topics of conversation until their listeners show some interest. Or it could also be that the process runs its course without the participants' awareness.[8]

Other experiments have shown that verbal reinforcement can be equally effective in changing more complex forms of behavior. In one study for instance, an experimenter transformed college students' normal styles of forming sentences by saying "good" whenever they happened to change their grammatical productions.[9] In another experiment, college students met in individual sessions with an experimenter who asked them to talk about anything that came to mind.[10] According to a prearranged plan, the experimenter said as little as possible, not even "uh-*huh*" or "is that so?" as one normally would to keep a conversation going, until the student began to talk about a particular subject matter, for example, about contemporary musicians. As the one-sided interaction started, however, the experimenter might say "uh-*huh*" if he thought the ongoing topic might in time lead to the one decided on in advance. If, for instance, the student started to discuss classical music, the experimenter would reinforce him once, but participate no further until the discussion turned to modern musicians. After that, talk about musicians and reinforcements for the talk would come thick and fast. A bit later, when the discussion of the desired topic was going full steam, the experimenter would extinguish the student by withholding his ap-

[7] See L. Krasner, "Studies of the Conditioning of Verbal Behavior," *Psychological Bulletin* 55 (March 1958): 148–70.

[8] See D. Dulaney, "The Place of Hypotheses and Intentions: An Analysis of Verbal Control in Verbal Conditioning," *Journal of Personality* 30 (June 1962): 102–9; C. A. Insko and R. B. Cialdini, *Interpersonal Influence in a Controlled Setting* (New York: General Learning Corp., 1971).

[9] H. Barik and W. E. Lambert, "Conditioning of Complex Verbal Sequences," *Canadian Journal of Psychology* 14 (March 1960): 87–95.

[10] W. S. Verplanck, "The Control of the Content of Conversation: Reinforcement of Statements of Opinion," *Journal of Abnormal and Social Psychology* 51 (November 1955): 668–76.

probation and, in a short time, the topic would change. Even opinions about campus issues and attitudes of various sorts have been modified systematically with the same procedure, and these modifications often do take place without awareness.[11]

These experimental studies demonstrate vividly how actions and thoughts are controlled and modified in the course of social interaction. It is not difficult to look beyond experiments and find support for this phenomenon. Consider the following excerpts from a character study of a famous American author, Thomas Wolfe, written by a professional writer who very likely never heard of Professor Skinner or his notions about reinforcement. And yet in it we learn that Thomas Wolfe wrote prodigiously as though he were being reinforced for writing, much as pigeons are reinforced for pecking rapidly, and he dwelt on certain topics much as the college students did in the experiment we just examined.

> Thomas Wolfe was a man obsessed by the act of writing. He wanted to make a complete written record of every experience he remembered, and there was never time enough for that; time was the enemy. With time at his shoulder he wrote "like a madman," "like a fiend," and "as if pursued by devils." . . . He was trying to produce a volcanic mountain of words as high as Parnassus. "It may be before I am done," he wrote . . . "that I shall say something important—that in the mad rush to get it down, something of high worth may come out."
>
> Meanwhile he kept quoting production figures, like the manager of a busy mine from which words were being drilled and blasted like lumps of anthracite. Thus he reported in 1926: ". . . I am writing about 3,000 words a day, which I hope to increase to 4,000 . . ." In 1933: "I have written over a million words in manuscript the past four years, which makes a box five feet long by two and one-half feet wide piled to the top." The seventy-five thousand words he claimed to have written in three weeks of June, 1934—by actual count there was less than one-half as many—were the story of his father's death that appeared in *Of Time and the River*, and they were among the best words of his brief career.
>
> He wanted to pour out everything he remembered in one torrential flood, but he also wanted to increase his reservoir of memories by going everywhere and doing everything . . . the desire to write had become "almost a crude animal appetite."[12]

This description suggests that in his early social relationships Wolfe may have been very effectively reinforced for expressing himself completely, so much so that his whole personality may have been marked

[11] Insko and Cialdini, *Interpersonal Influence in a Controlled Setting.*
[12] M. Cowley, "The Miserly Millionaire of Words," *The Reporter* (7 February 1957): 38–40.

by an abnormally intense need to communicate. If the details were available, it would be fun to compare Wolfe's background and experiences in social interaction with those of William Strunk, a grammarian who became renowned for his insistence on using the very minimum of words, of making "every word tell."[13] "Crude animal appetites" to express everything and tendencies to make "every word tell" are very likely established through patterns of reinforcements received over the years from others with whom we interact.

Patterns of reinforcement, in fact, become the central theme of a significant new work of Skinner in which he proposes a radical plan to change and improve society and man's place in it.[14] Put simply, he views man as nothing more than a complex system of behaviors, each element shaped by extensive social interactions beginning in infancy. Beliefs about man's putative freedom and dignity, he feels, are pretensions that stifle human progress. To improve his condition—actually, in Skinner's view, to survive as a form of life—man must decide and engineer his own future by planning and controlling just how he is to be shaped in the course of social and environmental interactions. Skinner argues that there are dependable ways of applying conditioning procedures that can redesign an entire culture, much as the experimenter and the pigeon through interaction created their own "culture."

SOCIAL INTERACTION AND
MUTUAL COMFORT

There are different, but not necessarily contradictory, conceptions of interaction. According to John Thibaut and Harold Kelley, social reinforcements determine the continuity as well as the disruption of social interaction.[15] At the start of a relationship, each participant shows various facets of his personality, carefully observing how the other reacts to them at the same time as he evaluates the recurring features of the other's personality. If the tryouts are mutually agreeable, or promise to be, interaction continues. If not, the relationship is broken. This trial period is sometimes hurried and comical, especially in planned get-togethers such as a freshman mixer at American coeducational colleges. After the newcomers are congregated—boys on one side, girls on the other—a boy typically takes a deep breath, a quick look, and then dashes toward a particular girl; she has been trained to gird her-

[13] W. Strunk and E. B. White, *The Elements of Style* (New York: Macmillan, 1959).

[14] B. F. Skinner, *Beyond Freedom and Dignity*.

[15] J. Thibaut and H. Kelley. *The Social Psychology of Groups* (New York: John Wiley, 1959).

self for such occasions. A brief interchange of conversation ensues during which both participants progressively turn on the charm. If one or the other turns it off, the boy moves on to try again with another girl.

What is it that makes social interaction mutually agreeable in some instances and disagreeable in others? Thibaut and Kelley find that if both participants are helpful or friendly, or if they express similar attitudes, the relationship has promise of continuing, since both persons receive rewards through the interaction. If, however, either participant increases the other's anxiety or shows hostility (for example, by refusing to be helpful), the budding relationship is likely to be extinguished because of the social "costs" incurred through the association. Interaction continues, then, if the rewards both participants receive from the relationship outweigh the costs involved. Associations between intimate friends provide many reciprocal rewards at low cost. These durable associations presumably provide a good deal of mutual satisfaction.

Interaction and the Theory of Social Systems

So far we have emphasized the mechanisms that get social relationships going more than the intriguing events that occur in the course of the relationships. Our purpose in this section is to analyze these events.

As Thibaut and Kelley demonstrate convincingly, people in social relationships do more than make deep psychological impressions on one another. Through their interaction they also become linked in a coherent social *system*. That is, their activities become interdependent so that actions on the part of one prompt reactions and readjustments from others. More than that, each interacting party learns not only how he should behave for mutual comfort, but also how the *other* is likely to behave. In social system terms, each party learns the *role of the other*. This double learning process has many implications for the study of personality and social systems.[16] For example, it provides A with the knowledge of how to behave like B if the situation later calls for that. These vicarious attempts to play the role of the other may or may not be directly reinforced. Perhaps this is how dependent children sometimes learn to become independent, how boys learn the roles of girls, how the loser learns to win.

When we think of interpersonal associations as social systems, we then see patterns of interactions between participants as being consistent and orderly processes that develop systematically. With this per-

16 G. E. Swanson, "Symbolic Interaction," in *The International Encyclopedia of the Social Sciences*, ed. D. L. Sills (New York: Macmillan, 1968), vol. 7, pp. 441–45.

spective, we would expect people who interact with one another regularly, as close friends do, to *adjust* to one another's ways of behaving, as elements in physical and biological systems do. Moreover, we would expect members of small groups to *react against* any member who threatens the existence of the group, as a psychological system reacts to changes in its equilibrium. In general, we would expect to find a regular and orderly *change* of interaction as social relationships develop or disintegrate. Let us examine the research evidence on interaction and see whether social relationships are indeed systematic.

MUTUAL ADJUSTMENTS IN SOCIAL SYSTEMS: PERCEIVED AND ACTUAL SIMILARITY

If social relationships are systematic, then participants should adjust to one another's ways of behaving. Theodore Newcomb, a proponent of the theory of social systems, suggests one important type of mutual adjustment likely to take place among people who establish comfortable associations.[17] People should adjust to one another's perceptions and attitudes, so as to make them as similar as possible. There are good reasons why this particular form of adjustment should occur. The more similar their perceptions and attitudes become, the more accurately participants can anticipate one another's ways of interpreting and reacting to new issues that arise. Furthermore, participants in social relationships are comforted by the feeling that their views are shared by others; if views are shared, they are believed to be socially correct. Thus, if their orientations are similar, members of a social system are brought closer together psychologically; to the extent that similarity facilitates interaction, their interaction becomes more efficient. According to the theory, participants in mutually satisfying relationships should adjust their perceptions and attitudes as interaction proceeds because of the advantages derived from similarity.

What evidence is there that mutual adjustments of perceptions and attitudes do take place? Joel Davitz carried out a simple but instructive study with ten-year-olds at a summer camp.[18] He found that campers who chummed around together and finally became close friends *perceived* one another as being more alike in interests and preferences than did those who had not become close friends. In actuality, though, their interests and preferences were really no more similar than were

[17] T. M. Newcomb, "An Approach to the Study of Communication Acts," *Psychological Review* 60, no. 6 (November 1953): 393–404.
[18] J. Davitz, "Social Perception and Sociometric Choice of Children," *Journal of Abnormal and Social Psychology* 50, no. 2 (March 1955): 173–76.

The value of being like people important to us

those of randomly selected pairs who had not become friends. In interpreting the findings, Davitz argues that people have a need to be similar to others they value and like. This need, he believes, is developed in childhood through experiences in imitating and identifying with parents and other important people in our lives. As children, we learn the instrumental value of being like people who are important to us and this value carries over into friendships as we grow older.

The tendency to distort perception to match our wishes is certainly not limited to children. Levinger and Breedlove, for example, found that the actual similarity of attitudes of husbands and wives is markedly less than the similarity thought to exist.[19] Thus, participants in social

[19] G. Levinger and J. Breedlove, "Interpersonal Attraction and Agreement: A Study of Marriage Partners," *Journal of Personality and Social Psychology* 3, no. 4 (April 1966): 367–72.

interaction can actually modify their views so that they will be more similar, or they can remain insensitive to actual differences and merely *think* others really feel as they do. Although both adjustments may be made that could contribute to similarity, sometimes the similarity is more apparent than real. In the case of apparent similarity, however, the functioning of the social system will be impaired. In this instance of apparent similarity, what would happen if the friendships continued for a longer period of time? Would the perceptual distortions ultimately disrupt the relationships, or would adjustive mechanisms come into play? Newcomb's research on the acquaintance process provides us with at least partial answers to these questions.[20]

With the assistance of the university administration, Newcomb invited seventeen men students, none of them previously acquainted, to live without charge in a student house on campus, managing their own meals and making whatever living and study arrangements they wanted. In return, they were to be available an hour or so each week to members of a research team who wanted to find out what their basic attitudes were and how the men got along together. One researcher, in fact, would live in the house as a counselor.

As the young men got to know one another, they established tentative friendships and in certain cases formed exclusive cliques. Over the course of the year, many of the quickly formed associations proved to be unstable, the composition of cliques changed, and new friendships emerged. Through interviews conducted at the start of the year and at regular intervals thereafter, the researchers were able to determine: (a) each man's attitudes towards various social issues, (b) his perceptions of how others thought, felt, and reacted with regard to the same matters, and (c) how much he liked or disliked each of the other house members. With this information, the researchers could study what role attitudes and accurate perceptions of others played in the formation of both short-lived and longer-term friendships.

Several modes of mutual adjustment came to light. As our analysis of attitudes in Chapter 4 would lead us to expect, young men of this age would likely be resistant to attitude change and, in fact, Newcomb found little change in their basic attitudes during the year. As tentative friendships were established, each member of a pair got to know a good deal about the other's attitudes. But when annoying differences emerged, the relationship dissolved and each person started new relationships with other friends. Acquaintanceships, however, developed into friendships only when those involved happened to have similar

20 T. M. Newcomb, *The Acquaintance Process* (New York: Holt, Rinehart & Winston, 1961).

profiles of attitudes to begin with. Merely thinking that each other's attitudes were similar was not enough to sustain an association over a long time span.

Those involved in the more durable friendships actually became more similar over the year in their evaluations and opinions of other house members. To this extent, then, close friends did adjust to one another's social perceptions. According to more recent research, similarities of attitudes promote and augment interpersonal attraction.[21] Thus, the close friends in Newcomb's study were likely drawn closer together psychologically as their social perceptions became more similar.

Newcomb provides us with an instructive overview of the development of social systems. Personal needs to seek out others with similar outlooks led to comfortable and satisfying friendships which, in turn, contributed to the cooperative management of affairs in the house.

DISSIMILARITY

The need for similarity among participants in social interaction is powerful, as we have seen, and its influence runs deep. For instance, there is an accumulation of evidence that people like people who like them.[22] (This principle holds up well except for the interesting case of people who have little self-esteem. Apparently it is difficult to really like someone who likes you if you have serious questions about your own worth. It is as if the person with little self-esteem asks himself: "What sort of judgment can *he* have if he likes a clod like *me*?") There is also good evidence that good-looking people are attracted to good-looking people. In social contacts with opposite-sexed partners who vary in degrees of attractiveness, people who aren't good-looking tend to choose each other.

But one can question the social values underlying these findings and the emphasis people seem to give to similarity. Are relationships established on the basis of similarity necessarily genuine, deep, constructive, and valuable? It is a healthy symptom of society if, as in Newcomb's study, people either distort their true feelings or else break up social contacts that prove to be based on dissimilarities of outlooks or on uncomfortable reward-cost ratios? An important counter-theory is being explored by those who question the value placed on similarity. Maslow and Izard, for instance, believe that independent or *self-actualizing* people are intrigued rather than threatened by the dissimilarities between

---

[21] See E. Bersheid and E. H. Walster, *Interpersonal Attraction* (Reading, Mass.: Addison-Wesley, 1969), especially chap. 6.

[22] Ibid., chaps. 5, 6.

themselves and their friends.[23] And Levinger argues that mature and productive human interaction is based as much on a *complementarity* as on a similarity of needs, values, and personality styles.[24] This important idea has also been applied to interaction in large complex social systems, such as industrial organizations, by Ziller and by Weick.[25] They argue that a sense of personal significance and value develops in human associations when people demonstrate what they can do as independent individuals. Rather than duplicate other people's roles, they need to be able to express their uniqueness, their differences. The point is that in social interaction people have antagonistic needs—needs for similarity as a means of belonging, and needs for dissimilarity as a means of maintaining individuality. One of the challenges of life is to learn to adjust to *both* these forces. And the problem of adjusting to the claims of both forces seems to apply to the functioning of informal groups and complex, departmentalized organizations as much as it does to the functioning of the individual.

REACTIONS TO DISTURBANCES IN SOCIAL SYSTEMS

If social relationships are systematic, then equilibrium-producing adaptations should appear when any one component causes disturbance in the system. In two-person systems we have seen that the association may dissolve when tension-producing difficulties arise. If mutual satisfactions cannot be obtained or if fundamental differences between participants come to light, the association all too often dissolves.

Here we shall examine similar adjustments that take place in a group when one member challenges the group's purposes. The example we will use is a now classic experiment by Stanley Schachter.[26] Schachter invited college students to join one of several "newly organized" campus clubs. He told them, for example, that a "case-study" club was being

---

[23] A. H. Maslow, "Love in Healthy People," in *The Meaning of Love*, ed. A. Montagu (New York: Julian Press, 1953); C. E. Izard, "Personality, Similarity, and Friendship: A Follow-up Study," *Journal of Abnormal and Social Psychology* 24, no. 6 (June 1963): 598–600.

[24] G. Levinger, "Note on Need Complementarity in Marriage," *Psychological Bulletin* 61 (June 1964): 153–57.

[25] R. C. Ziller, "Individuation and Socialization: A Theory of Assimilation in Large Organization," *Human Relations* 17 (December 1964): 341–60; K. E. Weick, *The Social Psychology of Organizing* (Reading, Mass.: Addison-Wesley, 1969).

[26] S. Schachter, "Deviation, Rejection, and Communication," *Journal of Abnormal and Social Psychology* 46, no. 2 (April 1951): 190–207.

organized at the request of local lawyers and social workers who were seeking advice on the treatment of delinquents. Interested students could also join "editorial," "movie," or "radio" clubs, each purportedly being formed to give advice to professionals. Clubs were subsequently organized, each comprising eight or so students with supposedly common interests. Without the volunteers' knowledge, however, Schachter placed two accomplices in each group. One was to be consistently deviant in the beliefs he expressed and the other, equally deviant at the start of the meeting, was to modify his views slowly until he was clearly in agreement with the others.

At the first meetings (in fact, the groups had only one meeting, after which the plan of the experiment was revealed), club members were asked to decide on matters of general policy and to iron out any differences of opinion. Each case-study club, for example, read through the record of a delinquent boy, and members exchanged views on how he could be helped. The deviators in each group expressed the view that the boy should be punished until he changed his ways—an opinion very different from the group's consensus.

The stage was then set to examine how the members would react to the deviators. The first development was a marked increase in communication directed to the deviators, a determined effort to convince them that their views were clearly inappropriate and to bring them back in line. This lopsided pattern of interaction intensified as the malleable deviator showed signs of changing his views. Near the end of the meeting, however, as it became clear that the stubborn one was a lost cause, communication with him promptly died away. He was ultimately shut out of the group and the others proceeded without him. For instance, as they discussed what committees should be set up, he wasn't even considered, and when members were asked to indicate in private who was and who was not valuable to the group, the stubborn deviators were unanimously rejected.

Although one can question again the value and the social utility of this pressure toward similarity, the overpowering pressure against deviance is unmistakeable in this example. Naturally, this pressure for similarity is not restricted to college students. The same effect has been found with high school students and with employees in department stores.[27] The point is that effective procedures emerge spontaneously in social interaction to counteract the disturbance created by one member whose deviance threatens the system's smooth functioning. The

27 B. E. Collins and B. H. Raven, "Group Structure," in *The Handbook of Social Psychology*, ed. G. Lindzey and E. Aronson (Reading, Mass.: Addison-Wesley, 1969).

trouble is, of course, that although a potential Hitler might be crushed by such pressure, a potential Einstein with really novel ideas might also be ruled out. And this important corollary will be examined in the next chapter.

THE ORDERLINESS OF THE
INTERACTION PROCESS

If social relationships are systematic, then interaction should proceed and develop in a regular and orderly fashion. The orderliness of interaction is very apparent in the work of R. F. Bales and his associates and they present us with a comprehensive theory of how social systems work. They also show us a methodology for observing and evaluating the interaction process of small groups in operation.[28]

Bales looks at members of groups as actors and reactors who become related to and dependent on one another through interaction. For him, interaction is the essential feature of groups—the mortar, so to speak, that binds people together in associations. In fact, Bales is convinced that the fundamental nature of a group can be explored by carefully analyzing interaction, much as an individual's personality can be fathomed by studying the network of his thoughts and feelings. If Bales were to eavesdrop on a conversation or bull session among friends or the deliberations of a formal group, he would note who had spoken to whom, who had reacted, who initiated new ideas, who kept the discussion on the track, who tried to change the topic, who generally agreed with others, who disagreed, and how frequently each person had acted or had been reacted to. Rather than record the content of statements, he would be mainly concerned with the purpose of each speaker's remarks and how these remarks affected the course of the discussion. For instance, in an informal discussion among girls, if one said, "I wonder how Muriel really feels about going out with Bill." Bales would record this as a *request for opinion* of others in the group. If another replied, in an unfriendly manner, "Oh, you and your questions. You're as inquisitive as Freud!" her statement would be classified as *showing antagonism*. If the first girl then blushed or otherwise showed embarrassment, her emotional reaction would also be recorded. Bales would eventually slip away with a full record of the sequence of actions and interactions among group members. With this information, he would make an amaz-

---

[28] See R. F. Bales, "Interaction Process Analysis," in *International Encyclopedia of the Social Sciences*, ed. D. L. Sills (New York: Macmillan, 1968), vol. 7, 465–71.

ingly comprehensive analysis of the group, determining how the inter-action progressed from moment to moment, which members became the centers of communication, who reduced tension and who generated it, and who were likely power figures.

As part of a planned study to determine who held the power in fam-ily matters, Fred Strodtbeck, a colleague of Bales, participated while a husband and wife discussed certain topics.[29] To evoke differences, he asked them to think about three families they both knew well and to give their individual opinions about which of the three had the hap-piest children. In many cases, as you might expect, the spouses dis-agreed, and in these instances, they were asked to discuss the matter and arrive at a common decision. Strodtbeck wondered whether there would be a systematic pattern of interaction from one couple to an-other, and whether husbands or wives would be more likely to give in so as to reach a common decision. Strodtbeck wondered whether there would be a systematic pattern of interaction from one couple to an-other, and whether husbands or wives would be more likely to give in so as to reach a common decision. He also wondered how a white Protestant American husband and wife would compare with Mormon and Navaho couples given the same questions to consider. He chose Mormons as a comparison group because in their culture women gener-ally play a subservient role to men, whereas other American women are believed to have equal rights with men. In Navaho culture, wives gen-erally play more influential roles than do their husbands.

On the basis of these cultural facts, Strodtbeck predicted that the outcome of the discussions would vary predictably from culture to cul-ture. Observing ten couples from each cultural group, he found that American men and women won about the same number of decisions, whereas Mormon husbands and Navaho wives were the more power-ful partners in their discussions. As to the patterns of interaction, Bales found that, for all three cultural groups, those who won the decisions were the most talkative members of the pair. Also, the more talkative persons asked more questions, gave more opinions, and showed more agreement with their partners who, in turn, were generally more pas-sive, except for occasional outbursts of hostile remarks. Thus, the re-sults indicate that the specific *outcome* of interaction was determined, at least in part, by the cultural background of the participants, whereas the *pattern* of interaction was, in general, consistent from one cultural group to another.

Bales and his associates have given special attention to small dis-

[29] F. L. Strodtbeck, "Husband-Wife Interaction Over Revealed Differences," *American Sociological Review* 16 (June 1951): 468–73.

cussion groups of six or so college students, previously unacquainted with one another. The groups are asked to discuss case studies of people facing everyday difficulties, to arrive at a consensus about the problem presented, and to suggest ways to ameliorate it. With these provisions, it is possible to observe the development of interaction from the start of a group's existence.

Drawing on his research with large numbers of such groups, Bales believes people join formal groups with two expectations in mind. First, members expect the group to achieve the goals for which it was created. Thus, a seminar group should educate, a recreational group should entertain, and a conference group should sift through facts and opinions and reach generally acceptable conclusions. Second, members expect to use the group setting to develop their own styles of associating with others, whether they are interested in being group leaders or merely passive, but well-liked, participants. The social system, then, must permit the establishment of a stable status structure and an integrated set of roles that members can play comfortably. Pressures toward these two ends are often antagonistic, and if either is given too much emphasis, the efficiency of the system is reduced; too much concern with either attaining group goals or with developing pleasant interpersonal associations can hamper the system's operation.

By carefully studying patterns of interaction, Bales determined how groups typically resolve this problem and ultimately satisfy both expectations.[30] In a remarkably systematic fashion, he found, interaction *alternates* between (a) one person's contribution to the discussion of the case material, and (b) the emotional reactions of others to his remarks. This alternation means that attention is at one moment directed to matters of goal attainment and at the next to matters of interpersonal association. To illustrate, suppose one member makes a suggestion about how the discussion should turn. There are two aspects of his action: he wants to move the discussion ahead (a goal-achievement pressure), but he also wants to direct the discussion according to his own plan, possibly hoping that others will look on him as the source of particularly good ideas. Others in the group react to his suggestion *and* to him by agreeing or disagreeing. They evaluate his idea, and then decide (by what amounts to a majority vote) whether they should accept it and thereby give him status credit in the group, or compete with him by presenting their own ideas. With each such decision, the group takes a step forward in establishing satisfactory role relationships and then

[30] See R. F. Bales, "Some Uniformities of Behavior in Small Social Systems," in *Readings in Social Psychology*, ed. G. E. Swanson, T. M. Newcomb, and E. L. Hartley (New York: Holt, Rinehart & Winston, 1952).

it redirects attention back to the case material. There are two points to note here: (a) that through interaction, members become interdependent in a coherent social system, (b) that through a regular alternation in the focus of the interaction, both types of members' demands are satisfied, enabling the system to capitalize on differences of viewpoint and to progress toward solving the problems presented.

To examine the sequence of interaction over a longer period, ten groups were reconvened for four separate one-hour meetings, studying a different case at each meeting.[31] As members got accustomed to one another, they spent less time in discussing the case material specifically and more in expressing feelings. Interpersonal communication apparently improved because the members accomplished their task requirements although less discussion time was spent on the subject matter. With experience, they also tolerated more disagreement and demanded less explicit agreement with one another's views. In fact, joking and friendly overtures replaced standardized forms of agreement.

During the second of the four sessions disagreement and hostile reactions to one another's views reached their peaks, as though a conflict of some sort (competition for group leadership, for example) was crystallizing. To check this possibility, the researchers privately asked group members to name the person they felt had been the best discussion leader after each of the four meetings. By the last meeting, members in four of the ten groups studied agreed on their leaders, whereas in six groups there were several contenders for leadership. For those groups with recognized leaders, the hostility and disagreement so prevelant in the second meeting clearly dissipated during the last meetings. For the groups with competition for leadership, the hostility continued throughout all four meetings. Thus, the *sequence* of interaction appears to follow an orderly course, despite conflict and stress in the system, even though the characteristics of the interaction are distinctively different in the two instances.

Bales's current work—an exciting new analysis of personality—is founded on the orderliness of the interaction process and the contributions each actor makes to it.[32] By looking through the grid of interaction networks, Bales is able to isolate each actor's more durable characteristics. One person may emerge as the key figure in whatever groups he enters because of the large number of communications he receives and sends; another may be admired for his contributions;

31 C. Heinicke and R. F. Bales, "Developmental Trends in the Structure of Small Groups," *Sociometry* 16 (March 1953): 7–38.

32 R. F. Bales, *Personality and Interpersonal Behavior* (New York: Holt, Rinehart & Winston, 1970).

one may emerge as an isolate who hardly ever participates; another may appear as domineering because he participates too much. Bales also examines the various coalitions that are likely to form on the basis of similarities and differences of interaction styles. It is in coalitions of various sorts that people try to enhance their power and compete for control over the interaction. The competition, of course, can be constructive or destructive.

ORDERLINESS OF INTERACTION AT THE MOLECULAR LEVEL

At the same time as Bales's work progresses on the more global aspects of interaction, other investigators are beginning to explore the more molecular features of the process, and already these appear to be just as orderly and predictable. One example of this recent work is that of Meltzer, Morris, and Hayes at Cornell on the interruptions that commonly occur when group members communicate.[33] Normally, members of groups take turns in presenting ideas and reacting to the ideas of others. The strand of interaction typically moves from member A to B to X to A, and so forth. But more often than we realize, members' communications overlap, so that A and C, for example, may both have the floor for brief moments (usually about one-third second), so that C's communication is momentarily interrupted by A's. The Cornell researchers wondered how overlapping is resolved in rapidly moving discussions. It turns out that the one whose argument is maintained during the overlap is most commonly the defender, not the interrupter, and the way he wins out is by raising his voice. Even if he is normally more soft-spoken than the interrupter, a slight rise in voice is the defender's way of demanding his right to continue, and he usually gets his way.

Adam Kendon's work shows that body language is another reliable accompaniment to interaction.[34] Kendon finds an intricate relationship between speaking and the automatic movements of head, arms, hands, and trunk. His research uses minute analyses of motion-picture frames of body movement coordinated with syllable-by-syllable breakdowns of speech. Kendon's work demonstrates that expressive body movements

[33] L. Meltzer, W. N. Morris, and D. P. Hayes, "Interruption Outcomes and Verbal Amplitude: Explorations in Social Psychophysics," *Journal of Personality and Social Psychology* 18 (June 1971): 392–402.

[34] A. Kendon, "Some Relations Between Body Motion and Speech," in *Studies in Dyadic Communication*, ed. A. Seigman and B. Pope (Elmsford, N.Y.: Pergamon, 1972); A. Kendon, "Movement Coordination in Social Interaction: Some Examples Described," *Acta Psychologica* 32 (March 1970): 1–25.

are integrated facets of each act of communication. The positioning of body parts appears to take place just before a major speech or thought unit is produced; the new posture is held throughout the course of such a unit, with slight changes in the positions of head, arms, and hands being made to accompany smaller units of thought and speech. The speaker's gestural changes seem to indicate the direction of his thought and the important features of the message. What is amazing is that the listener tends to coordinate his body and to change his posture with the speaker, almost as a mirror image. Thus the listener seems to get into step with the speaker as though he must take on the role of the speaker in order to comprehend more completely. The listener will get out of step with the speaker when he has listened enough and wants the floor himself; his movements are a signal to the speaker to stop talking.

In Perspective

Social interaction is the process by which people influence one another through mutual interchange of thoughts, feelings, and reactions. First we examined the process from the perspective of the learning theorist, presenting the argument that interaction gets underway and continues when participants receive something they need or want through associating with one another. This principle of need satisfaction seems to hold as well for rudimentary forms of symbiotic relationships as for more complex social interactions. Starting with the socialization process in infancy, the modes of behavior and personality traits of those in social interaction are molded, in part, by mutual reinforcements. The disruption of interaction also depends on social reinforcements. Interaction continues as long as all participants find it worthwhile; if not, relationships are broken—unless their continuance is coerced—and more satisfying ones are formed.

From another point of view, people in social relationships become linked with one another in a social *system*; that is, their activities become interdependent so that one person's actions prompt reactions and adjustments from others. When this concept of social systems is examined carefully, it becomes clear from research examples that those in interaction do adjust to one another's behavior, that members of social systems do react strongly against anyone who threatens the group's existence, and that the pattern of interaction develops and changes in an orderly, systematic fashion. The systematic nature of the process is as evident at the more molecular levels of analysis as at the more molar levels.

Social interaction is the concern of many disciplines. It is evident from the theory and research findings now available that our current and future knowledge about the process depend on the interaction of psychologists, social psychologists, and sociologists, who have social interaction as a common interest.

The Individual in
Group Settings

chapter six

Our purpose in this chapter is to examine the psychological consequences of belonging to groups. The more we can learn about this fascinating topic, the better we can understand a whole area of behavior
that otherwise remains mysterious. For instance, why is it that most
people anxiously adapt their actions and even their ways of thinking
to what they believe others expect of them? At the same time, how
is it that certain individuals view groups as opportunities to lead rather
than follow, to set standards of behavior rather than conform to them?
As we examine various psychological effects of participation in groups,
we shall also demonstrate through research examples how the behavior
of individuals is often dramatically affected by very subtle changes in
the ways groups are organized. Then we shall examine how attachments to groups develop normally, and how these attachments sometimes become overdeveloped and lead to intergroup conflicts that are
extremely difficult to resolve. In the final section the analysis will lead
to a consideration of a highly personal type of intergroup conflict that
we all face when our allegiances to different groups are inconsistent.
We will see that conflicts of allegiances are especially frustrating for
immigrants or members of ethnic minority groups who feel unsure

photo by Bob Brooks

about group membership and who often wonder if, in fact, they belong at all.

Throughout, we shall have in mind the definition of a *psychological group*: two or more individuals who, through social interaction, depend on one another to play distinctive roles in the pursuit of common interests or goals. Thus, a family, a circle of friends, or club associates are all psychological groups because the interacting members have developed expectations of how others should behave in the pursuit of common objectives. Congregations of unacquainted people or mere collections of students, however, are not psychological groups (even though it is common practice to refer to collections of subjects as experimental groups or, simply, groups). In certain instances we shall compare psychological groups with mere collections of people in terms of their impact on the behavior of individuals.

The present discussion will draw on concepts already developed in previous chapters. It will become apparent, for example, that group membership affects social judgments and attitudes, and that various factors of socialization contribute to individual differences in reactions to groups. In particular, we shall explore further the concept of social interaction as we examine how groups affect individuals.

But there is something special about the topic of this chapter, and it has to do with awareness. While discussing interaction, we tried to bring to light various subtle processes that usually remain implicit. For instance, we are not normally aware of being influenced by the social reinforcements of others nor do we purposefully reinforce others in our everyday interactions, even though behavior can be socially controlled, apparently without awareness. Neither are we cognizant of being an element in an interdependent social system when we interact with others. In contrast, we are much more aware of being influenced and regulated by the expectations of the groups we belong to; we know what we should not do in certain social settings and what we must do in others. When it becomes apparent to us as children that we can't explain everything to our parents or even to our gang, when we begin to notice the changes in our own behavior as we come to the front of a class to recite, when we conform in our styles of dress, hair, or speech, or when we avoid being an "odd-ball," we are thereby acknowledging social standards that limit and stereotype our behavior. But being somewhat more aware of the powerful influence of groups does not mean that we understand how groups affect our behavior. In fact, the psychological effects of group membership are only now beginning to be understood because of recent advances in the behavioral sciences. Hopefully, it will be entertaining and instructive to study a sample of these new developments.

The Psychological Effects of Participation in Groups

SOCIAL FACILITATION

The psychology of groups really got started about 1920 when Floyd Allport, wondering about the effect of groups on individual behavior, conducted a series of experiments.[1] Using college students as subjects, he tested association of ideas and soundness of arguments, comparing the number and quality of ideas generated when subjects performed in

[1] F. H. Allport, "The Influence of the Group Upon Association and Thought," *Journal of Experimental Psychology* 3 (1920): 159–82.

groups and alone. He found that the presence of others energized individuals (he used the term *social facilitation*) at the same time as it cut down on the quality of thinking. Although he concluded that work demanding concentration or original thinking would be better done in solitude, his conclusions about the principle of social facilitation cannot be generalized to all groups, as we shall see. But it was with research of this sort that Allport awakened the interest of psychologists and stimulated them to develop better methods of studying the behavior of individuals in various group settings. Contemporary researchers look more carefully into both the social structure of the group in question and the personality traits of its members. They also give attention to a broader spectrum of behaviors that may be modified in group settings.

Allport's basic ideas, despite their vagueness, are still matters of great concern. His notion of social facilitation has recently been reformulated and translated as a *socially induced distraction of attention*;[2] and it has been reinterpreted as a state of *arousal* (a neurophysiological level of activation) pushed beyond an optimal point.[3] Of course, these recent modifications of the basic idea have taught us a great deal, for example, that the sheer presence of others often calls out particular social motives that inhibit and distract. We also have learned that this form of social distraction fortunately wears off with time.

THE STANDARDIZATION OF BEHAVIOR

Since Allport's early work, a large number of experiments have been conducted in which individuals, either alone or in groups, were asked to make all sorts of estimates—the lengths of lines, the sizes of rectangles, the number of beans in a bottle, the number of clicks heard, or the amount of apparent movement of a tiny spot of light in a dark room. It turns out that the judgments of individuals in group settings characteristically become more alike, tending to cluster around an average judgment. That is, those who made more extreme judgments when alone tended to make judgments according to a group average in the presence of others. Muzafer Sherif argued that this movement toward a group average or *norm* was due to the development of a shared frame of reference for what constitutes appropriate and expected behavior.[4] For example, group members are likely to adjust their actions to the trend set by a group leader, since they see a leader as an originator of

2 H. H. Kelley and J. W. Thibaut, "Group Problem Solving," in *The Handbook of Social Psychology*, ed. G. Lindzey and E. Aronson (Reading, Mass.: Addison-Wesley, 1969), vol. 4, chap. 29.

3 R. B. Zajonc, "Social Facilitation," *Science* 149 (1965): 269–74.

4 M. Sherif, *The Psychology of Social Man* (New York: Harper & Row, 1936).

group standards or an exemplary exponent of them. In experiments on this question, Sherif noted that once the group member had shifted toward the average, this group norm would prevail even if the leader tried to start a new standard by changing his original estimate. The norm, then, apparently has an autonomous power and individuals regulate their behavior with reference to it.

However, these demonstrations of the importance of group standards are not fully convincing because they are typically concerned with perceptions of the magnitude, number, or movement of physical objects. Do group standards affect psychological functions other than judgments and perception? Would individuals' attitudes shift toward a group average when influenced by the discussion of others? This problem was examined by Lambert and Lowy in a study with McGill University students.[5] In their study, psychological groups were compared with groups of unacquainted students. Antidemocratic attitudes were measured by different forms of the *F scale* (fascism scale), administered first when the individuals were alone, then when they were in the presence of others but instructed not to talk, and a third time when they were together and free to communicate about the questionnaire before giving their attitudes. Control subjects completed the three forms of the questionnaire at three different times, but always alone. With students who were well acquainted, it was found that attitudes clearly converged toward a group average when measured either in group settings that allowed communication or in settings where members sat next to one another but were not permitted to talk. Furthermore, the attitudes of the group as a whole became significantly *more democratic* in the together-but-no-talk condition, but they bounced back to the original level when discussion was permitted. Apparently, in trying to zero in on the attitude norm in the no-talk phase they made an inappropriate estimate that had to be revised because of the discussion. In contrast, unacquainted students were unperturbed by either the presence or the discussion of others. Their attitudes did not change any more than those of the control subjects.

These results suggest that people modify their attitudes, or at least the expression of their attitudes, if some personal advantage follows from a change. Students who were well acquainted probably derived benefit and comfort from these friendships, and they could doubtless estimate the acceptable range of attitudes for the group by merely noticing who was sitting with them, without discussion. Anticipating that their attitudes might well come up for discussion when the experimenters had gone, the students may have guarded against appearing

[5] W. E. Lambert and F. H. Lowy, "Effects of the Presence and Discussion of Others on Expressed Attitudes," *Canadian Journal of Psychology* 11 (March 1957): 151–56.

deviant, since deviance could threaten their standing in the group. For those who were asked to give their attitudes in the presence of others they would not likely meet again, there was apparently nothing to be gained from a change, no matter how different they might be.

Kurt Lewin was one of the first to see the implications of the effects of group standards on attitudes.[6] He believed that individual attitudes can be more effectively modified by changing group norms than by attempting to work directly on the individual. In this way, the acceptable range of attitudes for all members of the group could be changed in a desired direction, whereas changing one person's attitude might unduly alter his standing in his group, making him deviant in the eyes of the other members. Rather than be alienated, the individual might well revert to his old attitude. It is very difficult for a single individual to go against a group.

GROUP-INDUCED SHIFTS IN ATTITUDES
AND DECISION CHOICES

The example just cited suggests that, although the presence of others prompts individuals to congregate their reactions around an estimated standard, the standard need not be a conservative or neutral one. In fact, our example showed the situation where a group shifted toward a more extreme attitude. Two researchers in France, Moscovici and Zavalloni, examined group influence in more detail and concluded that the group functions as a *polarizer* of attitudes.[7] In the "alone" condition, French students' attitudes toward President De Gaulle were on the average slightly favorable while attitudes toward Americans were slightly unfavorable. But after a group discussion of these attitude topics, the group reactions shifted toward the extremes, attitudes toward De Gaulle becoming more favorable and those toward Americans becoming more unfavorable. Moscovici and Zavalloni believe that several factors may cause this effect: (a) subjects become more involved in the group setting; (b) the task may become more meaningful; or (c) subjects could become more certain of their positions.

This interesting study reminds us that group settings can just as well radicalize ideas as it can temper or neutralize them. Researchers must now determine what it is about groups that promotes moderation in some cases and polarization in others.

Another fascinating form of group influence on individual judgments

[6] M. Deutsch, "Field Theory in Social Psychology," in *Handbook of Social Psychology*, ed. G. Lindzey and E. Aronson (Reading, Mass.: Addison-Wesley, 1969), vol. 1, chap. 6.

[7] S. Moscovici and M. Zavalloni, "The Group as a Polarizer of Attitudes," *Journal of Personality and Social Psychology* 12 (June 1969): 125–35.

is known as the *risky shift*. When subjects are asked to make decisions about real-life dilemmas, they are much more likely to make a riskier decision after a group discussion of the issues than when they decide alone. The shift toward risk is a strong and reliable one for a whole class of choice-dilemmas. For example, should Mr. A, married with one child, leave a secure job for another with a very uncertain future but with greater possibilities of partnership? Should Mr. B. chance a delicate heart operation that could, if successful, completely relieve a serious heart ailment? Should the quarterback in the final minute of a game chance a play that could break the tie or, if unsuccessful, cost his team the game?

A very lively research campaign is now going on to explain this socially important and theoretically significant effect, as well as to discover which discussion items lead to greater riskiness or greater conservatism.[8] At this time, some findings support and some findings cast doubt on a large number of explanatory attempts. Researchers are now concerned with such problems as the following: Is the risky shift due to a diffusion of responsibility for the group-based decision? Is it that members' choices on some items are based on cultural values about taking risks that are made more salient in a group setting? Is it that members want to show themselves in public as more risk-taking than they really are? What group conditions, or what topics, encourage conservative opinions?

CONFORMITY

There has been a progressive refinement in psychological interpretations of the group's effect on the individual since the 1920s. Currently, researchers' interests have moved from the formation of group standards to a more precise analysis of individual reactions to standards, that is, to the phenomenon of conformity.

Imagine that you are asked to participate in an experiment along with seven other college students. You are all called together and a professor explains that you are to look at certain displays of straight lines and say which one in a set is the shortest, calling out your answers one at a time. Suppose you happen to be sitting at an end seat around a large table and are the last to express a judgment. The first card shows three lines, one of which is clearly the shortest, and all eight of you say so. On the next card, you are again sure that one line is plainly the shortest, but you hear each of the others indicate another line. You don't realize that the other group members are paid accomplices of the professor who have been coached to make certain wrong

[8] D. G. Pruitt, "Choice Shifts in Group Discussion: An Introductory Review," *Journal of Personality and Social Psychology* 20 (December 1971): 339–60.

choices in a convincing manner. The idea is to pressure you to conform. As each person declares his judgment, your incredulous smile meets serious countenances of the others. When it's your turn, how would you react?

Judging from Asch's results, only about 42 percent of Swarthmore students maintain their opinion against the incorrect majority while many go along with the majority despite their own certainty.[9] Asch interviewed each critical subject after the experiment and found that only a tiny minority actually saw the incorrect line as being shortest. Most yielders saw the lines one way but began to doubt their perceptions. Others yielded out of fear of appearing different; they disregarded what was right or wrong and paid attention only to what they should say in order to agree with the majority.

Interestingly enough, variation of this experiment established that a majority of three was as strong an influence group as seven or more. However, when a naive subject was supported by one other person against a majority of accomplices, the conformity effect was markedly reduced.[10]

Richard Crutchfield has transformed the basic procedure so that a number of critical subjects can be observed at one time.[11] In Crutchfield's setup, as many as five individuals at a time are seated in private booths, each with its own display screen. A slide might appear on each screen showing a standard line next to several comparison lines, with response keys to indicate which line is shortest. Another slide with the statement "It is necessary to suspend free speech in times of crisis," invites the subject to indicate agreement or disagreement by pressing an appropriate key. While each person believes that he can read from a panel of lights in his own booth the answers others are giving, the experimenter actually controls the sequence of lights in all booths. As in Asch's procedure, each subject is sometimes instructed to wait until the others have responded before giving his own answer, and on these critical trials he believes the others have agreed on what to him is an incorrect answer.

Crutchfield found that 30 to 70 percent of adults conformed to the group consensus on certain critical items. When attitudes were put to

[9] S. E. Asch, *Social Psychology* (Englewood Cliffs, N.J.: Prentice-Hall, 1952).

[10] Because subjects are being deceived in these experiments, social psychologists reveal the deception as soon as possible after the investigation and explain the full purpose of the research. The phenomenon being studied can only be captured in a normal setting, which often requires a deception. When informed, subjects characteristically express respect for the methodology and the significance of the findings because they have experienced their own involvement. Even so, there is concern in our field that deception may be used too much and many researchers are seeking alternative procedures.

[11] R. S. Crutchfield, "Conformity and Character," *American Psychologist* 10 (February 1955), 191–98.

this test, about 30 percent yielded to a false group consensus. For instance, to the statement "I believe we are made better by the trials and hardships of life," almost no one in a control group disagreed, whereas 31 percent did when under group pressure. Even personal doubt is brought out by the technique. When asked, "I doubt whether I would make a good leader," over 30 percent of men who were potential leaders in their professions were pressured to express uncertainty about themselves.

In another experiment, Crutchfield used the technique to probe attitudes toward socially relevant issues. He asked subjects for their views toward such issues as "Free speech being a privilege rather than a right, it is proper for a society to suspend free speech whenever it feels threatened." Faced with a false group consensus that apparently agreed with this sentiment, three times as many subjects went along with the group as would have had they been asked privately. In these examples, the social significance of the effects of group pressure becomes obvious.

Crutchfield noted large individual differences in the extent of conformity—some persons submitted 17 times out of the 21 critical trials, others yielded only once. Crutchfield then examined various personality characteristics of his subjects, using well-established measures of personality traits, and correlated these with extent of conformity. It turned out that the independent person, in contrast to the conformist is more intellectually effective, more mature, more confident, and less rigid or authoritarian. The two groups also have decidedly different attitudes toward parents and children. The conformists tend to idealize their parents, whereas the independents are more objective and realistic, both praising and criticizing. Furthermore, the conformists are more restrictive in their attitudes toward child training, the independents more permissive. Note that the traits characterizing the conformist are very similar to those that characterize the authoritarian personality (see Chapter 4). Just as the development of authoritarianism can be traced back to early childhood experiences, perhaps as research progresses we shall also be able to discover more of the roots of conformity.

Some recent studies suggest that one deep root of conformity is affiliation need: people with strong personal needs for affiliation are particularly prone to conform in Asch-type social situations.[12] Support for this interpretation comes from the investigations of Walker and Heyns who argue that conformity is a way of behaving that helps a person to be accepted and liked by others.[13] In their studies, they found that the extent of conformity depends on the attractiveness of membership

[12] A. Mehrabian and S. Ksionzky, "Models for Affiliative and Conformity Behavior," *Psychological Bulletin* 74 (August 1970): 110–26.

[13] E. L. Walker and R. W. Heyns, *An Anatomy for Conformity* (Englewood Cliffs, N.J.: Prentice-Hall, 1962).

in a particular group, that is, on the social rewards derived from belonging. A person will conform to norms in those groups he wants to be accepted in, and he will become a nonconformist, thereby showing his rebellion, in groups he does not find satisfying. But since most people want to be accepted in at least some groups, it follows that nearly everyone, regardless of personality style, can be made to conform when the situation is right. Thus it is becoming evident that the final account of conformity will have to deal with *both* personality traits and situational factors.

The final account must also consider the *depth* of conformity. In some cases there is only a surface compliance with group pressure while in others compliance is based on a genuine acceptance of the group influence. Charles and Sara Kiesler stress the importance of the distinction between simple compliance and private acceptance.[14] For instance, they present evidence to show that strong pressure to comply may force people to go along with the group but have little effect on private acceptance of the influence attempt. Extreme pressure, in fact, can boomerang: an individual's private attitudes may become more opposed to that of the group's.

AUDIENCE ANXIETY

The active social interplay of group members is not the only influence on the behavior of individuals. People are also influenced by the passive and silent group members in much the same way as an actor is affected by the mass of faces that constitutes his audience. In fact, one can think of social life as a series of entrances on different stages where "lines" are recited before audiences that vary in degree of expertness, of size, or of importance for the actor. A project by Wapner and Alper tried to capture this idea, using undergraduates who were asked to "perform" before audiences of varied composition.[15] In one case the audience was unseen, but the students realized that people were watching and listening to them. In another, the audience—a faculty member and several students—was actually visible. In a third condition, there was no audience, except for the experimenter. The subjects' task was to select appropriate words to complete certain phrases. Hesitancy in responding was found to be greatest with the unseen audience, and least with the experimenter alone. The point of the study is that our behavior varies from one audience to another, and we are likely

---

[14] C. A. Kiesler and S. B. Kiesler, *Conformity* (Reading, Mass.: Addison-Wesley, 1969).

[15] S. Wapner and Thelma Alper, "The Effect of an Audience on Behavior in a Choice Situation," *Journal of Abnormal and Social Psychology* 47 (April 1952): 222–79; Kelley and Thibaut, "Group Problem Solving."

to become constrained and cautious if we have insufficient information about a particular audience.

One's liking or disliking of an audience is not a simple matter only based on whether or not listeners agree with what one has to say. Harold Sigall's recent research shows that a speaker prefers an audience that disagrees, then changes its opinion according to the argument, rather than an audience that politely agrees but makes no attitude change.[16] Our reactions to audiences, then, depend on how much the audience is affected by our communication.

Why do so few people really enjoy the limelight? Most of us experience at least some degree of stage fright. As noted in Chapter 2, Paivio has been able to trace back individual differences in degree of audience anxiety to particular types of child-training experiences.[17] As research on this problem progresses, our understanding of many aspects of the effect of groups on the behavior of individuals will be advanced.

NONCONFORMITY AND LEADERSHIP

Individuals differ greatly in their reactions to the group. Some are extremely anxious before audiences, and some are very quick to conform to group standards. But not everyone conforms to norms, nor does an individual conform in all groups he is associated with. In fact, some people view social groups as opportunities for setting standards rather than adjusting to them, for being themselves rather than conforming, for leading rather than following. What are the qualities that characterize nonconformists and group leaders?

Social psychologists have considered this question from several points of view. Hollander, for instance, believes that an individual must earn the right to be a nonconformist.[18] If the nonconformist's novel or unconventional suggestions for group action have proven valuable to other members in the past, the group gives him idiosyncrasy credits. That is, he is given the opportunity to express his ideas because others believe it is to their advantage to listen to him. If his ideas require adjustments on the part of others and prove unsuccessful, he uses up his credits and is then expected to keep his ideas to himself and to listen to the proposals of others. In other words, he is then expected to let someone else try his hand at leading. A certain few are able to accumu-

16 H. Sigall, "Effects of Competence and Consensual Validation on a Communicator's Liking for the Audience," *Journal of Personality and Social Psychology* 16 (October 1970): 251–58.

17 A. Paivio, "Childrearing Antecedents of Audience Sensitivity" (Ph.D. dissertation, McGill University, 1959).

18 E. P. Hollander, "Conformity, Status, and Idiosyncrasy Credit," *Psychological Review* 65 (March 1958): 117–27; E. P. Hollander, *Leaders, Groups, and Influence* (New York: Oxford University Press, 1964).

late a large reserve of idosyncrasy credits, thereby earning the privilege to make decisions for the group. Thus, a person can develop the reputation of having good ideas and become a group leader.

Leaders of this sort have been studied by R. F. Bales, using the techniques of social interaction analysis that we examined in the last chapter.[19] Bales finds that leaders are motivated by a strong desire to control the activities of others while keeping themselves free from outside control. Although this role may bring them a certain type of respect, much as efficient specialists are given respect, according to Bales, they are unlikely to earn affection. If, instead of overplaying the specialist role, a person remains sensitive to the needs of others and helps them express their ideas, he may become the most-liked person in the group. According to Bales, it is very unlikely that one person can play both the best-idea and most-liked roles in any one group. In fact, two distinct types of leaders usually emerge in most groups. The most-liked leader appears to be motivated by strong needs for affiliation and affection.

Sigmund Freud found this type of leader particularly interesting. In a fascinating little book on the psychology of groups, Freud argued that a leader emerges in a group when others find in him an object of affection.[20] Because they all experience a similar feeling for the leader, group members are drawn psychologically close to one another. The person striving to be most-liked, then, will be a successful leader if he manages to keep himself at the center of the information network and maintains the bonds of affection that unite the group members.

The nature of leadership is complex. An individual may confidently strive for one type of leadership in a particular group and be a passive conformist in another. Certain settings may call out the leadership potential of many group members, whereas in the other contexts no one will make a bid to lead. Fred Fiedler is of the opinion that the context or situational factors outweigh personality characteristics in determining who will be an *effective* leader.[21] He believes that in certain group contexts anyone can be an effective leader, whereas in other situations no one can lead effectively.

There is something refreshing about Fiedler's approach. Many young people today worry about the leadership role because a strong leader usually means passivity for the rest of the group. Fiedler suggests that

---

[19] R. F. Bales, "Interaction Process Analysis," in *International Encyclopedia of the Social Sciences*, ed. D. L. Sills (New York: Macmillan, 1968), vol. 7, pp. 465–71; R. F. Bales, *Personality and Interpersonal Behavior* (New York: Holt, Rinehart & Winston, 1970).

[20] S. Freud, *Group Psychology and the Analysis of the Ego* (London: Hogarth Press, 1922).

[21] F. Fiedler, *Leadership* (New York: General Learning Corp., 1971).

the leader mystique can be profitably replaced by rotating the leadership role among group members. Then each member's aptitudes may be drawn on for the solution of special problems.

Psychological Effects of Variations in Group Organization

So far we have emphasized how behavior is affected by participation in groups without giving much attention to variations in group structure. Groups, of course, differ in their organization. Some are formal, others informal; some are autocratically structured, others democratically; some are cooperatively formed, others competitively. People are clearly aware of the differences in group *atmosphere* associated with such organizational variations even though they may not be cognizant of how their behavior is affected by such differences. Social psychologists have been active in examining how subtle changes in a group's organization do affect, often dramatically, not only the actions of individual members but also the performance of the group as a whole. This research trend is our present concern.

VARIATIONS IN THE FORM OF
GROUP COMMUNICATION NETWORKS

Social groups differ in the degree to which a member is free to communicate with others. Some are so formally structured that each person should communicate only with those immediately above or below him in the hierarchy. Others are organized around one or two people who function as a communication center, receiving requests and giving out information. Still others are informal and permit free communication among all members. According to the network used, some members feel that they have central positions in the group and others feel they are in fringe positions.

Alex Bavelas and Harold Leavitt have developed a means of examining variations in group communication networks and observing their effects on the behavior of participants.[22] They created an experimental analogue for various patterns of communications that commonly develop in both small groups and in large complex organizations. For instance, they limited the ways in which five-person teams could communicate

---

[22] A. Bavelas, "A Mathematical Model for Group Structure," *Applied Anthropology* 7 (1948): 16–30; H. J. Leavitt, "Some Effects of Certain Communication Patterns on Group Performance," *Journal of Abnormal and Social Psychology* 46 (March 1951): 38–50.

while attempting to solve problems that called for the transmission of information throughout the group. Although each member initially received a certain clue to the problem, the group had to examine all five clues before the problem was solvable. To exchange information, each subject was required to write messages and pass them on to certain others in the network. Four network patterns were used: a circle, a straight line, a Y, and an X. The arrangements of the five members can be diagramed as follows:

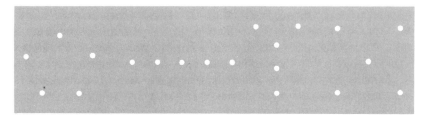

In the circle pattern, each person was permitted to communicate with those on either side of him. In the straight line, the same rule held, except that communication was limited for the people at each end, since they had only one other next to them. In the X pattern, the four members at the corners communicated with the man at the intersection who, in turn, could pass information back to each of them. The two men on the fork points of the Y pattern could only pass information in to the man at the juncture. With all patterns except the circle it is clear that certain positions will be central and others peripheral to the flow of information. The structures also vary in their organizational flexibility. For example, the circle gives all members an equal chance to take charge whereas the X pattern virtually assures that the man at the juncture will be the information center.

Leavitt and Bavelas were interested in the effect these network variations would have on the speed and efficiency of problem solving. It turned out that groups in the circle and line structure in contrast with those in the X and Y patterns were less efficient in that they used more messages to reach solutions. Yet when errors were made in the circle network, they were able to be corrected more easily. Thus, although the circle is inefficient in one sense, it still provides more opportunities for all members to learn how to communicate, a condition that could be advantageous with subsequent problems. Furthermore, when subjects were asked how much they enjoyed taking part in the experiment, those who worked in the circle pattern were the most satisfied, possibly because of the greater freedom provided by the circle's organization. The circle pattern affords the most independence of action for all members, the least likelihood that leaders will arise, the least stability of organization, and, clearly, the fewest feelings of being peripheral.

The early work of Bavelas and Leavitt has been greatly expanded over the past twenty years, but one consistent difference among networks is that between centralized (the X and the Y) and decentralized (the circle) patterns.[23] Although the decentralized networks facilitate solutions to more complicated problems confronting a group, the centralized networks facilitate solutions to simpler problems.[24]

UNORGANIZED AND ORGANIZED GROUP STRUCTURES

In a now classic study, John French compared the behavior of individuals in unorganized and organized groups.[25] The unorganized "groups" were assemblies of college undergraduates who were not acquainted with one another before the experiment; the organized groups were college athletic teams and established clubs from the community. The groups were given problems to solve, some of an intellectual nature, others requiring coordinated motor performances of all members. Although the problems looked easy enough, they actually were very difficult or insoluble. For instance, one intellectual problem was actually impossible: members were required to fill in rows and columns of numbers that would add across and down to a certain sum. The solution of a coordination problem was possible but very improbable: each member was to take one of the handles of a large cone-shaped apparatus and try, in unison, to roll a small ball up a path from the base to the top. French was interested in determining how the differently structured groups would respond to the frustration these tasks would generate. The subjects were instructed to work together as teams in their attempts and to switch problems if any proved difficult.

As we might expect, the unorganized groups showed various signs of disruption and lack of interest as their attempts failed. They broke up into pairs or subgroups working in isolation on one problem or another, or even on matters unrelated to the experiment. And yet it was the organized groups that had the greater number of minor disruptions. They apparently were more deeply frustrated, for they directed more

[23] B. E. Collins and B. H. Raven, "Group Structure," in *The Handbook of Social Psychology*, ed. G. Lindzey and E. Aronson (Reading, Mass.: Addison-Wesley, 1969).

[24] M. E. Shaw, "Communication Networks," in *Advances in Experimental Social Psychology*, ed. L. Berkowitz (New York: Academic Press, 1964).

[25] J. R. P. French, "The Disruption and Cohesion of Groups," *Journal of Abnormal and Social Psychology* 36 (April 1941): 361–77.

aggression toward one another and the demands of the experiment. Because they were among friends, they may have felt freer to express themselves. Their common interest in doing well as a team kept them focused on the problems, but it also made them more emotionally involved. French argues that members of the organized groups were motivated not only by the demands of the experiment but also by a group-shared desire to do well as a team.

There are advantages and disadvantages, then, to group organization. The mutual attraction of members in organized groups sustained their motivation to succeed and kept them functioning as a team. These characteristics, of course, could be of great advantage in many circumstances. But groups that are too well organized might suffer from a lack of flexibility in adjusting to frustration or to danger. Information from French's work pertains to this point. As we have seen, more hostility and frustration seemed to be expressed in the organized than the unorganized groups. In another phase of his experiment, French put organized and unorganized groups to work on various tasks in separate rooms of an old building. After a short time and according to plan, the building seemed to be on fire and as the subjects tried to get out, they found the doors were firmly locked.[26] Of course, the smoke piped in under the doors and the sounds of fire engines were all part of the experiment. One might expect the organized groups to attack the problem in some orderly fashion, but actually fear and near panic appeared to spread more rapidly among the more organized groups.

What, then, would be an optimal degree of group organization? Too little social organization is worrisome because it comes very close to the anonymous, impersonal, detached way of life found in big cities where people develop the habit of keeping out of other people's affairs. The current research on *bystanders*—those who passively watch victims in distress—addresses itself to the lack of organization, pushed too far.

Darley and Latané have arranged experimental analogues of real-life bystander situations.[27] In one investigation, subjects were kept busy in a room while from next door they heard the calls for help of an employee obviously in pain. When alone, most subjects were quickly moved to investigate and offer help, but when working with strangers, the horrible tendency was to sit still and ignore the cries for help. Why is it harder to act responsibly when responsibility is shared? Current studies have found that the presence of bystanders who are not associ-

[26] J. R. P. French, "Organized and Unorganized Groups Under Fear and Frustration," *University of Iowa Studies in Child Welfare* 20 (1944): 229–308.
[27] J. M. Darley and B. Latané, "When Will People Help in a Crisis?" in *Readings in Social Psychology Today* (Del Mar, Calif.: Communications Research Machines, 1970).

ated with one another socially certainly influences behavior, so much so that bystanding can become contagious.[28]

DEMOCRATICALLY AND AUTOCRATICALLY STRUCTURED GROUPS

An important investigation into the effects of variations in group structure was carried out by Kurt Lewin and his colleagues in the late 1930s.[29] They wanted to create different social climates for groups of eleven-year-old boys by varying how the adults supervising the groups performed their roles. The democratic supervisor called the boys together and asked them what they would like to do with the time and resources available to them in the experiment's clubhouse. Although he was the leader, he really became a member of the group. With shirtsleeves rolled up he worked, played, and went along with agreed-upon plans as any other member did. In contrast, the authoritarian supervisor called his group together and described what each member should do and how he should do it. He watched the boys attentively and informed them what to do at each step.

It turned out that the authoritarian structure promoted a great deal of hostility, usually directed to scapegoats in the group, but never to the supervisor. Apathy, lack of motivation, and dependence on the supervisor became the major characteristics of the authoritarian groups. The autocratic leader was the communication center, so to speak, but the communication was limited to club activities and was more formal than spontaneous. The democratically organized groups, in contrast, were freer in communication. Members made more statements using the pronoun "we," gave more suggestions for policy matters, and displayed more affection for their leader.

These variations in leader-controlled group atmospheres clearly and differentially affected the functioning of the whole social system. The effects were noticeable in the *type* of communication (which ranged from hostile to friendly), the *direction* of communication (among all group members in one case, toward or from the supervisor in the other, and the *amount* of communication (from apathetic silence to a bombardment of suggestions).

---

[28] S. H. Schwartz and G. T. Clausen, "Responsibility, Norms, and Helping in an Emergency," *Journal of Personality and Social Psychology* 16 (October 1970): 299–310.

[29] K. Lewin, R. Lippitt, and R. K. White, "Patterns of Aggressive Behavior in Experimentally Controlled Social Climates," *Journal of Social Psychology* 10 (1939): 271–79; R. K. White and R. Lippitt, *Autocracy and Democracy* (New York: Harper & Row, 1960).

Is this finding universal? Robert Meade wondered if in a relatively authoritarian culture the democratic structure would still be so obviously superior.[30] He arranged a replication of the Lewin study in northern India with groups of Hindu boys working with either a democratic or authoritarian leader. Over a six-week period it was found that morale and the quality as well as the quantity of work completed all favored the authoritarian atmosphere. These outcomes, so different from the American ones, suggest that young people brought up in a comparatively authoritarian society are more accustomed to and comfortable with an authoritarian work-group atmosphere.

COOPERATIVE AND COMPETITIVE
STRUCTURING OF GROUPS

In an experiment with college students, Deutsch created cooperative or competitive classroom atmospheres by varying the information students received about the course makeup.[31] Instead of taking a regular course in psychology, they would meet in small seminars focused around the analysis and discussion of real-life case studies. The competitive classes were told that each student would be ranked from best to worst in terms of skill in analysis and discussion, and that each person's final course grade would be an average of his daily ratings. The cooperative-group members heard that the major part of their course grades would depend on the quality of discussion shown by the whole group. Note what these instructions mean to each individual. In the cooperative setting, individual and group goals are made identical, attention is shifted away from the self to the interaction of all members, and any tendency to shine is tempered by the realization that one's contribution should move the total social system along toward the goal of effective analysis and discussion. The competitive group members, however, were set to look out for themselves since their course grades depended on their individual skills.

These instructional differences made remarkable differences in performance. The cooperative groups developed into psychological groups; the competitive groups did not. Cooperative groups not only produced more ideas per unit of time but the quality of ideas was also found to be superior. Compared with members of the competitive groups, their

[30] R. D. Meade, "An Experimental Study of Leadership in India," in *Comparative Perspectives on Social Psychology*, ed. W. W. Lambert and R. Weisbrod (Boston: Little, Brown, 1971).

[31] M. Deutsch, "A Theory of Cooperation and Competition," *Human Relations* 2 (March 1949): 129–52, 199–232; see also A. J. Smith, E. Madden, and R. Sobol, "Productivity and Recall in Cooperative and Competitive Discussion Groups," *Journal of Psychology* 43 (June 1957): 193–204.

members were better able to communicate with one another, showed more integration of one another's ideas, were more friendly, and were far more satisfied with the group's performance. For example, more cooperative-group members took on tasks of regulating and integrating the discussions, while the competitive-group atmosphere was marked by attempts to dominate and seek personal recognition.

Deutsch's experiment demonstrates nicely how skilled individuals are at switching their whole style of behavior—for example, from a concern with self to concern for others—when reward is made contingent upon such a change. And once a spirit of cooperation or of competition spreads, the performance of the whole group is markedly affected. But one wonders whether Deutsch's experiment may not have over-emphasized cooperation. Karl Weick gives us some perspective on this possibility.[32] He argues that people become more involved in and satisfied with groups that provide opportunities for competition as well as cooperation, that is, opportunities to alternate between *socialized action* and *individualized action*. Weick believes that groups can deal effectively with change only when both the cooperative and the competitive propensities of man are encouraged. Researchers very likely will start testing Weick's ideas.

Nevertheless, the investigations of Bavelas, French, Lewin, and Deutsch all show that one's style of behavior is sensitive to changes in social atmosphere caused by changes in group organization. When the organization maximizes each member's feeling of being important, encourages free communication, generates a democratic or cooperative social climate, it then provides opportunities to all members to play distinctive and comfortable roles in the pursuit of common interests and goals. In other words, groups can be structured to foster the development of psychological groups in which individual differences can be expressed.

Instructive as these basic researches are, they may nonetheless seem too academic and theoretical to be of practical value in today's fast-moving world. We can expect a shift in research emphasis toward application; there are already some signs of this. For example, social psychologists are beginning to ask if there are group structures that keep consistency between attitudes and behavior specifically to the fore. Churches do so, but only in a diffuse way. Perhaps student movement groups will be more effective because they provide supportive structures powerful enough to coerce members to act forthrightly on their values and attitudes.

[32] K. W. Weick, *The Social Psychology of Organizing* (Reading, Mass.: Addison-Wesley, 1969), p. 105.

The Psychology of Intergroup Conflict

People normally develop loyalties and a sense of pride in their groups, a feeling that their groups are better in some respect than comparable ones they are not associated with. Whether or not these feelings are justified, group members are affected by them. In certain cases group loyalty unites and sustains the members in great accomplishments. But because group pride is often supported by negative comparisons with similar groups, it is a potential source of rivalry and conflict whenever groups come in contact. In fact, much of the conflict we observe between neighborhood gangs, religious groups, and nations is based on exaggerated feelings of group pride. We cannot explain such instances of intergroup conflict by merely extending our knowledge of intragroup interaction. Rather, we need information about actual social contact between groups and the effects of such contact on the behavior of group members.

A group of psychologists led by Muzafer Sherif have initiated programs of research into group rivalry and conflict.[33] These investigations do not answer all possible questions about intergroup conflict, but the methods and theory used to study the problem are extremely promising first steps.

The researchers used a three-phase experiment. They first invited twenty-two eleven-year-old boys from a large Oklahoma community to spend three weeks in a private summer camp. Acting as camp directors and counselors, the psychologists were able to observe the boys constantly and to interview them at regular intervals during the three-week period. The boys were previously unacquainted with one another, but they had been selected because they all were socially well-adjusted and intellectually bright youngsters from comfortable middle-class homes. The campsite was ideal for the realization of each phase of the experiment. For instance, it was large enough so that the twenty-two youngsters could be separated into two groups, each with its own camping and athletic facilities, and far enough apart that the groups might never come in direct contact.

The first phase of the plan called for the parallel development of two distinct, cohesively organized groups. During the first week, the boys in each group prepared their own meals, decided on schedules of activities, and organized various athletic events. These experiences per-

---

[33] M. Sherif et al., *Intergroup Conflict and Cooperation: The Robbers Cave Experiment* (Norman: University of Oklahoma Institute of Group Relations, 1961); M. Sherif and C. W. Sherif, *Groups in Harmony and Tension* (New York: Harper & Row, 1953).

mitted close friendships, stable hierarchies of members, and leaders to develop in each group. Within a few days, group slogans, flags, and favorite songs became marks of group solidarity in both camps. By the end of the week, two solid psychological groups had developed. According to plan, "chance" contacts between groups had occurred during the first eight days. For example, the groups "just happened" to pass each other on hikes, and the water carriers from both groups happened to meet at the spring. Within the week, members of both groups insisted on meeting the others in competitive games.

This spontaneous clamor for contact, especially for competitive contact, was the sign the psychologists had been waiting for before going on to the second phase: to bring the groups together in competitive activities, encouraging the competition to develop into conflict. The period of intergroup contact started by arranging a series of baseball games, tug-of-war and tent-making contests—activities that would necessarily lead to victory for one group and defeat for the other. Friction between the groups became progressively apparent. Both groups resorted to derogatory slogans and hostile acts such as messing up the other group's cabins. During the second week, it became clear that the time had come to turn off the heat. But the experimenters were apprehensive about this third phase because, in an earlier study where conflict was brought to the boiling point, they had not been able to completely resolve the hostilities.

The first strategy in the conflict-reduction phase was to arrange especially pleasant surroundings whenever the groups were brought together (an application of the association principle). They had the best meals of the summer and saw the most enjoyable movies together in each other's presence. But when these attempts proved to be generally ineffective in reducing the tension, the experimenters used another ploy. They now tried to arrange situations where the cooperative efforts of all twenty-two boys would be required—situations, that is, that would force a merger of groups. The theory was that individuals could be diverted from their group allegiances if they could see advantages in a merger. Perhaps they would trade membership in the smaller group for membership in a more efficient *superordinate* group. To implement this idea, the boys were taken on a day's outing in two separate trucks, one for each group. While the boys were swimming in their own swimming holes, the experimenters hid one truck in the woods and left the other in a spot between the temporary campsites and placed the heavy tug-of-war rope beside the truck. After the swim, the boys returned to their tents, ready for lunch. The truck driver said he would go for food, but according to plan, the truck would not start. Members of both groups watched the strained efforts of the driver as he repeatedly tried to get the motor to turn over. Then one boy suggested they try to pull the truck with the rope to get it rolling. It was evident that all the available manpower was needed and that, without the truck, no one would eat. All twenty-two boys joined in, and after several attempts they got the truck rolling and the motor started. Group differences were overlooked during this episode and all the boys were visibly satisfied with their joint accomplishment. From that point on, there was a regular increase in friendly intergroup contacts, supported by a series of planned situations calling for intergroup cooperation. There were occasional relapses to separate group activities, initiated by certain fellows who felt they might lose status in a merger, but these relapses failed to catch on and became less frequent. Within three days, there was convincing evidence that a new superordinate group had been formed and the two former groups had been dissolved.

With this study, Sherif and his associates have not only demonstrated that intergroup conflict can be examined systematically, but they have also shown how readily people can form allegiances to their groups and how easily conflicts can develop. Their means of reducing conflict, although it has important practical implications, was a radical one because two cohesive groups were broken up in the merger. Could they have reduced the conflict and still left the groups intact? Is it possible for groups to interact harmoniously and yet maintain their separate identities? These are fundamental questions about intergroup relations that will likely receive much research attention in the future.

The Psychological Effects of Multiple-Group Allegiances

All of us belong to many groups and normally we find no difficulty in adjusting our ways of behaving to fit the expectations of one group or another. Sometimes, however, we find ourselves in settings where the influences of two groups overlap and we face a conflict in adjusting to incompatible demands. For instance, the boy who is dutiful and obedient in the family group but a tough and demanding leader of the neighborhood gang would be caught in a conflict if his parents should meet him by chance when he's out with the boys. Which role should he continue to play? Which group allegiance should he favor? More serious conflicts of this sort are commonplace for immigrants or members of cultural minority groups who, because of special experiences at home and different experiences outside, often wonder how to behave. In many cases, they are not certain which cultural group they belong to or whether they really belong to any. Is there some way that conflicts of allegiances can be resolved? Can an individual belong to two cultural groups simultaneously? In other words, can an individual develop comfortable bicultural identities?

In 1943, Irving Child examined a dilemma faced by many second-generation Italian young men in a New England community: were they Italian or American?[34] From childhood on, they had learned that they had lost contact with other youngsters in their community whenever they displayed signs of their Italian background, that is, whenever they behaved as their parents had taught them to. On the other hand, if they rejected their background, they realized they could lose the many satisfactions of belonging to the Italian community. Child noted three typical modes of adjusting to this conflict. Some rebelled against their Italian background and made themselves as American as possible. Some rebelled the other way, rejecting their American heritage as much as possible while proudly associating themselves with Italian customs. The third type of adjustment was that of the boys who apathetically withdrew from thinking of themselves in ethnic terms of any sort. Those who took this path tried unsuccessfully to escape the problem by avoiding situations where the matter of cultural background might come up, or by denying that there were any basic differences between Italians and Americans. In short, some tried to belong to one group or the other, and some, because of strong pulls from both sides, were unable to belong to either.

Although we are introduced here to the difficulties faced by people who are kept on the margin of two groups, there is no evidence presented to suggest that second-generation Italians can actually feel themselves a part of both groups. In 1962, Lambert and Gardner studied another ethnic minority in New England, the French-Americans, and observed many of the reactions Child had noted among Italian-Americans.[35] But there was one important difference.

By means of a series of attitude scales, Lambert and Gardner examined the allegiances of French-American adolescents to both their French and American heritages. The degrees of their skill in French and English were used as a behavioral index of their mode of adjustment to the bicultural conflict. In their homes, schools, and community, they had ample opportunities to learn both languages well, but whether they capitalized on the opportunities, it turned out, depended on their allegiances. Those who expressed a definite preference for the American over the French culture and who negated the value of knowing French were more proficient in English than French. Members of this group, moreover, expressed an anxiety about their progress in English. This subgroup's general rejection of their French background resembles in many respects the rebel reaction noted by Child. A second subgroup expressed a strong desire to be indentified as French, and they

34 I. Child, *Italian or American? The Second Generation in Conflict* (New Haven, Conn.: Yale University Press, 1943).

35 W. E. Lambert and R. C. Gardner, *Attitudes and Motivation in Second-Language Learning* (Rowley, Mass.: Newbury House, 1972).

showed a greater skill in French than English, especially in comprehension of spoken French. A third group apparently faced a conflict of cultural allegiances for its members were ambivalent, preferring certain features of both French and American cultures. Presumably because they had not resolved the conflict, they were held back in their progress in both languages when compared with the other groups. This unsuccessful mode of adjustment is strikingly similar to the apathetic reaction Child observed in a subgroup of Italian-Americans

A fourth subgroup is of special interest. Particularly intelligent French-American young people who were inquisitive and unprejudiced in their attitudes toward foreign peoples profited from their experiences with both languages and became fully bilingual. These young people had apparently surmounted the conflict and developed strategies to achieve a comfortable bicultural identity. Child had not noticed this type of adjustment in his study, perhaps because there are essential differences in the social pressures encountered by second-generation Italians and French, or perhaps because in the twenty years since 1943 the heat has been turned down under the American melding pot, the bicultural loyalties are more acceptable.

Suppose young children were given a thorough training in a second language and an immersion in a second culture by attending school taught by teachers from another cultural background. What impact would this experience have on the children's identity and cultural outlook? Improbable as it sounds, a long-term community study of just this sort has been conducted with English-speaking Canadian children who took their kindergarten and first grade schooling from French teachers who spoke French exclusively.[36] Beginning at the second-grade level English language training was introduced but kept to a minimum. But even with this minimum, the children were able to keep up in all aspects of English language skills with English-speaking children in control classes who followed a conventional all-English school program. What they had been learning in French was readily transferred to English.

But what is more interesting is that, by the end of grade five, the French-trained children had become sufficiently competent in French to be able to communicate naturally with French people and to establish close friendships with French children their own age. They had, in other words, become accepted in French spheres of social activities either as visitors or potential members of French social groups. In the process, they also developed favorable attitudes toward French peo-

[36] W. E. Lambert and G. R. Tucker, *Bilingual Education of Children: The St. Lambert Experiment* (Rowley, Mass.: Newbury House, 1972).

ple and French ways of life (European as well as Canadian versions) so that they thought of themselves as being *both* English- and French-Canadian. Without losing any English-Canadian identity, they had picked up a second identity effortlessly. Had they become comfortably bicultural? Yes, in the sense that they become at ease in both cultural settings they had learned the essential contrasts in what was expected of them in each type of setting, and they felt identified with both cultural networks. Is there really much more to being bicultural?

These investigations reveal how important group membership can be, especially when one feels one has to choose between groups. The studies also offer hope to those who see a social value in maintaining diverse cultural identities and in developing bicultural competence.

In Perspective

Our purpose in this chapter has been to explain the psychological consequences of participation in *psychological* groups—those comprised of two or more individuals who, through social interaction, depend on one another to play distinctive roles in the pursuit of common interests or goals.

Although we are vaguely aware of the powerful influence of groups, we normally do not realize how much we behave according to what we think the group norms are. In examining conformity, we noted that those who design their research to determine the importance of long-term personality dispositions find support for their position as do other researchers who feel that short-range influences from the immediate environment play the crucial role in determining who shall conform. Theoretical differences of this sort will undoubtedly lead to more comprehensive research into the effects groups have on individuals. But not everyone conforms to group standards. Some, it turns out, use groups as occasions to lead rather than follow, to set standards rather than adjust to them.

In pursuing our investigation of groups, we gave a good deal of attention to the various ways groups may be organized, and to the effects very subtle changes in the structure of groups can have on the behavior of those involved. Then we examined how group loyalties develop and how these can so easily become exaggerated and lead to stubbornly durable conflicts between groups. In the final section we considered a special form of intergroup conflict—the personal conflict of allegiances commonly faced by those who are unsure about their group membership, who wonder which group, if any, they really belong to.

Culture and Social Psychology

chapter seven

In this little book we have introduced a few of the recurrent processes that social psychologists study, such as socialization, attitude development and change, judgement of social events, group formation, and communication.

These processes are caught up in, and become a part of, the great and powerful sociocultural processes that are the stuff of social change and that make up so much of history. Economies develop and decline, revolutions come and go, religions and values develop and change, forms of expression in the arts and sciences become flexible or freeze into outmoded dogmas, structure of social relationships appear to group and divide. These are recurring sociocultural processes with which we are so very much involved in the twentieth century.

A Large Question

This leads us to a very large question we shall deal with in this chapter: What is the relation between these *sociocultural* processes and the *social-psychological* ones already considered? As you can well imagine, this

photo by Doug Wilkinson

question probably has several correct answers, and generates many disagreements.

THREE ANSWERS TO THE LARGE QUESTION

Our own answer to the large question really consists of three somewhat different ones, for there are at least three ways in which social-psychological matters relate to sociocultural ones. Two of these we shall discuss briefly, and the third we shall discuss at greater length.

Our first answer states, simply, that social-psychological processes are often dependent on and often caught up in the occurence of the larger sociocultural processes. If there is a change in the law regarding racial integration in public schools (a sociocultural event), then concurrently, or consequently, many attitudes are changed, many new acquaintanceships are formed, the socialization of many children (and adults) is changed, new perspectives in the judgment of social events develop, new groups and new norms emerge. These social-psychological processes appear to be caught up in the mainstream of the great sociocultural process of a change in the law. There is no doubt that it is often valuable to view social-psychological occurrences as caused by and captured by the widely shared events studied by sociologists and anthropologists, economists, and political scientists.

This first answer—that processes, like attitude change, occur in a captured or dependent manner in relation to sociocultural events and processes—leads many social scientists to feel that social psychology has little to offer on larger questions. That people change their minds as a result of a new law or a new election or a revolution is interesting but of no causal importance. Attitude change, for example, is merely a by-product of the great social processes. It is merely the squeak that is made by the social machine, so to speak. But social psychologists generally believe that even when one of their favorite processes *starts* from a larger social event, knowledge about the process will help to fill in the probable course of events as they flow from the molar level down to the final level of impact upon small groups and individuals. Knowing the details of the chain of events provides suggestions for social psychologists as to where to measure and evaluate change, and also provides more opportunities for benevolent intervention.

There is a second answer to our question, however. This second answer is that the great sociocultural events can be understood better if they are viewed as a macrocosm of the social-psychological processes. Talking about the occurrence of massive sociocultural events is often merely a convenient way of talking about combinations of various smaller social-psychological events. That is, that the very stuff of which sociocultural events is made is often social-psychological, as when a legislative act reflects the changing attitudes and social perceptions of legislators or judges, and when the enforcement of the new law depends upon the slow-changing habits and values of citizens and policemen. Diplomacy and politics are also the complex interactions of persons and attitudes; economic development depends on changing people's attitudes and decisions; innovations and revolutions often are the results of new social perceptions or attitudes of a small number of human actors. To believe in democracy is to recognize that the welfare of the many may be threatened by the willfulness of the few. Yet we also recognize the social-psychological nature and the human quality of great institutions when we judge the success of a democracy by the degree to which it defends the rights of minority groups as well as individuals.

Much research in social psychology is motivated by this second answer. Social psychologists concentrate all their knowledge to examine the fine texture of social and cultural events. When a social norm develops in a small experimental group in a social psychology laboratory, the gain in knowledge may apply to analyzing what goes on when parliaments debate, cabinets decide, union locals vote, or citizens go to the polls. There *may* be such a gain, but it is not yet certain. Only when we apply our knowledge of the microcosmic events to the actual macrocosmic events can we check out the value of social psychology for the study of larger social issues. We also need to learn much more about how smaller processes summate or otherwise contribute to create the noticeably macrocosmic processes.

This brings us to a third answer to our large question: Social-psychological processes are causally important as events that *mediate* or *integrate* the sociocultural events and processes. This third answer can be important whether or not we believe that society and culture are made of social-psychological stuff. We can view the relationship of the sociocultural and the social-psychological using a famous historical example. When the Volstead Act was passed by the United States Congress (a sociocultural event that may have resulted from a set of sociocultural processes), its success depended on a great many people changing their attitudes toward drinking alcoholic beverages. If the attitudes (and social habits) changed so that people disapproved of the habit, then the law was able to be enforced (which is another sociocultural process); if not, the law remained unenforceable. In this historic example, the social-psychological events did *not* follow the new law and enforcement, therefore, did *not,* and presumably could not, follow without enormous cost.

Let us use the issue of women's rights as a more contemporary example to show the relationship between sociocultural and social-psychological events. Unless some deep-seated attitudes and habits change as a result of the congressional decision to outlaw the unequal treatment of women in America, then the enforcement of the decision will continue to be slowed or defeated. The change of attitudes and habits is causally vital in this (and probably all) social change: the change or lack of change in attitudes permits or halts the expected larger social process.

This third answer to the large question seems the most satisfactory. Although it recognizes much of the wisdom in the other answers, it does rule out the notion that social-psychological processes are *always* by-products of social processes. This third answer also recognizes that social-psychological processes are often caught up in, or caused by, sociocultural ones; it further recognizes that social-psychological processes or events, by being causally linked to sociocultural events, may serve to mediate or to integrate aspects of the larger social world.

Figure A provides a simple graphic illustration of what we are talking about. It is quite easy to go beyond our schematic example and put one's social scientific imagination to work with additional cases and examples. Sometimes the process starts "above the line" in Figure A; sometimes it may start "below the line," as when a change in attitudes or values or expectations spreads widely, long before such a change is institutionalized by law. Perhaps the change in our attitudes toward the environment is such a case. Perhaps the quiet spread of alternative life styles is another process that begins with changes in the way individuals choose to spend their time, and spreads by imitation and other social-psychological means until changes in individual attitudes eventually lead

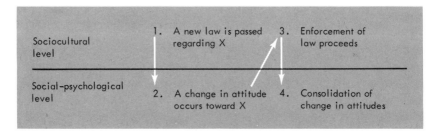

FIGURE A

to institutional changes. Sometimes, as in Figure A, there are one or two steps in the process, but often we must imagine numerous steps; sometimes it may be useful to increase the number of levels from two to three or more to systematically trace the development of great or small issues. We may want, for example, an additional level of opinion leaders or of individuals below the line, and additional levels of regions, nations, or international events above the line.

In passing, we should point out additional conceptual possibilities implied in Figure A. Some conceptualizations of social events operate "above the line." Structural or molar analyses of social events are often the preference of those who believe that social-psychological processes depend on the larger sociocultural processes. These analysts consider that social-psychological processes are outside their frame of reference.

It is also possible to analyze social issues from a perspective "below the line." A psychologist, for example, concerned with social issues from the perspective of the individual, may dismiss the importance of molar processes, or reduce them to their psychological meaning. To these analysts who view social issues from "below the line," the passing of a new law merely starts the really important attitude change process, and the procedures of law enforcement are merely rewards and punishments that effect the social learning processes of individuals. But there is at least some heuristic value in keeping Figure A in mind as we look at some of the studies that relate social psychology to sociocultural events.

Most of the truly systematic work on this problem of relating social psychology to the events of the larger society has involved the analysis of *past* cases. Although this is a sensible starting point for evaluating some of our social-psychological principles, we are now beginning to move on to consider *future* changes in societies or in social-psychological and psychological processes and events.

Let us look at some recent research attempts, and then return to consider the chicken-or-egg nature of causal analysis in this context. Our aim is to discover useful systematic order, not necessarily to deal with historical ultimate causes.

Personality and Economic Development

David McClelland, a Harvard social psychologist whose work on achievement motivation was discussed in Chapter 2, has extended his research to the sociocultural realm.[1] He argues that the *economic development* of a country is, in part, a social-psychological process, since it is highly correlated with a cultural pattern of early independence training and a high need for achievement. With these social-psychological components, the society can then strive for greater ecomonic development. We can simplify some of McClelland's ideas as follows:

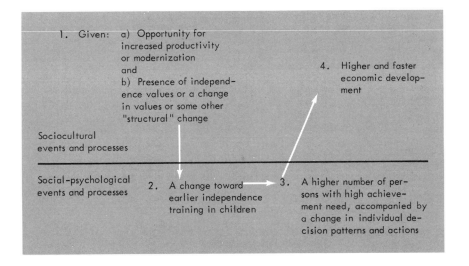

FIGURE B

Let us note at once that McClelland is not saying that the social-psychological factors can operate alone to encourage economic development. Economic opportunity and aid are also necessary. The point is that development often *fails* to occur or to be consolidated because the sociocultural conditions that favor the development of achievement motivation are not present. Development does tend to occur when these conditions are

---

[1] See David McClelland, *The Achieving Society* (New York: Van Nostrand Reinhold, 1961).

present, that is, when the correct *shared* values, or a change in values, or a structural change in the educational system occurs that, in turn, sets off the social-psychological events and processes below the line in Figure B. Then parents and teachers move toward emphasizing earlier independence training in their formal and informal relations with children. This creates greater need for achievement in more children. This need for achievement encourages a higher level of achievement, calls forth standards of excellence of performance, and fosters some degree of risk-taking. These motives encourage government officials to be efficient and businessmen to make industry hum.

McClelland's bold argument gives prominence to social-psychological factors in an important area of human affairs, and McClelland presents many kinds of research findings, most of which are inconsistent with his causal argument. Each of the relationships represented by the arrows in Figure B has been directly or indirectly investigated.

The relationship represented by the first arrow has usually been approached by studying the already existing value systems, including religious values, of various subgroups in America or Europe and relating them to child-training practices. The relationship represented by the second arrow has been studied by relating the history of a child's independence training to the strength of his achievement motivation, as we outlined in Chapter 2. McClelland has also checked the implications of this hypothesis. He reasoned that if a society tends to emphasize early mastery and self-reliance in a child, then the myths or stories of the society will carry themes relating to achievement.

You should note the strategy of proof here. McClelland is providing an array of evidence that agrees with or *converges* on the implications of the theory, rather than resting on any one study for his proof. He does so for two reasons: (a) it is impossible to experimentally alter societies in ways that would test his theory; (b) his hypothesis is very broad and inclusive enough, he feels, for all periods of history and all countries.

It is therefore sensible to test for *what would be expected to hold if the theory were correct* in the economic history of various nations. McClelland has done so ingeniously and persuasively. For example, he counted the occurrence of achievement themes in the orations read at the funerals of ancient Greeks; we can view such a count as a measure of item 1 (or alternatively of 3) in Figure B. It is possible to measure item 4 in the figure, at least indirectly, by noting the changes over the years in the distance from Athens that Greek vases were found—changes reflecting the expansion and contraction of Greek trade. When the measures of achievement motivations and economic expansion are related to each other over time, an interesting pattern emerges. The height of economic expansion occurs several generations *after* the achievement imagery has been at 'its height, and the decline in economic expansion occurs some time *after* the achievement imagery has fallen. The economic growth and decline, then, is possibly caused by the changes in the values or motivation of the people as reflected in the funeral orations of the time. The economic decline, McClelland suggests, may have been occasioned by an increase in the use of slaves to rear children during the wealthy period. Pampered children may not have been trained toward early independence; thus, there was a decline in achievement motivation.

Although McClelland has done similar studies on many other great historical empires, his most practical findings come from contemporary studies. In studying the relationship between items 1 and 2 in Figure B, he shows that people in the United States or Europe who adhere to the Protestant Ethic (which involves a personal relationship to the deity, self-advancement, and self-perfection) tend to train their children toward early independence. McClelland shows, more importantly, that if the children's school reading material is filled with signs of achievement striving (an indirect measure of childrearing practices), then *in the next generation* society will enjoy a greater increase in economic productivity.

McClelland leans heavily on his argument here. Although the need achievement in children's readers in 1950 cannot be predicted from the economic position of the country in 1925, it is possible to predict economic growth (as of 1950) from the need achievement in children's readers in 1925. It is even possible to predict somewhat the economic growth from 1950 to 1958 from similar (1950) measures of children's readers in a manner that cannot be predicted from strictly economic data. The proof of this argument is indirect because the measure of achievement motivation is not taken from children themselves nor is it taken directly from the child-training practices that McClelland believes precede high personal achievement motivation. Indirect or not, however, the evidence is impressive that social-psychological processes (the motivational basis of imagery contained in reading matter) are consistently interwoven with an important sociocultural process such as economic growth. McClelland's findings are also consistent with—even if they do not crucially prove—the kind of causal sequence outlined in Figure B. Crucial proof of causal relations in this realm of culture and personality is frequently sought but rarely achieved. McClelland's work, however, has the great value of suggesting that if a society wishes to expand economically, it should evaluate its human resources in terms of deep and early achievement motivations and it should reorder family life accordingly, as well as increasing economic opportunities. In short, cultural change and social-psychological processes may often be causally linked as Figure B illustrates.

Research on these problems of economic change constantly progresses.[2] Our diagram would have to be made more complicated if we were to try to contain all the systematic information now available. We would particularly need to complicate the relations represented by the first arrow of Figure B by emphasizing findings like those of Guy Swanson which demonstrate that Protestantism (during the Reformation) won out in European towns or centers where power was less centralized so that more people had a chance to get ahead.[3] McClelland emphasizes that where open competitive structures permit the reward of self-reliance, achievement motivation is encouraged. Higher levels of achievement motivation occur in Russia and China who (at least at the moment of revolutionary reform) believe that their systems are better than other systems in that they *originated* the ideological reform of world communism.[4] Countries such as Poland and Bulgaria display low need achievement (in children's readers), in part because they accepted their ideology from outside rather than having generated it themselves.

McClelland has also brought additional motives into the picture. In 92 percent of the fascist regimes (like those of Hitler, Franco, Stalin) the children's readers showed a high level of *need power* and a low level of *need affiliation*. Only 18 percent of democracies showed such a pattern. Research is being pushed toward showing the rise and fall in these various levels of national motivation. The United States, for example, peaked in achievement level in 1890 (followed by a slow, gradual decline to 1950), then peaked in need power around 1910, whereas need affiliation peaked in 1930. This sequence appears to occur more frequently than any other in the histories of nations. Soon we will be able to expand Figure B to include fluctuations of these various motives, and others as they are discovered.

Personality and Expressive Cultural Models

Human games and pastimes have fascinated both anthropologists and social psychologists for a long time. Games are part of a people's culture and general style of life; yet, at the same time they attract a good deal of individual, spontaneous involvement. The careful study of games should, therefore, provide insights into both the people and their culture, and some of the insights have begun to emerge from the systematic

[2] D. C. McClelland, *Motivational Trends in Society* (New York: General Learning Corp., 1971).

[3] G. E. Swanson, *Religion and Regime* (Ann Arbor: University of Michigan Press, 1967).

[4] McClelland, *Motivational Trends in Society*, p. 16.

Games as tension-reducing devices in our culture

collaborative work of John Roberts, an anthropologist, and Brian Sutton-Smith, a psychologist.[5]

These researchers believe that games *model* important aspects of culture and at the same time serve to *express* the needs of the people who choose to play them. Games and—in an even more removed sense—folk tales and music are an important case of a larger class of *expressive models*. Games also have two functions besides that of relieving boredom. They provide a way of teaching people (particularly the young) some ways of getting important things done; they also provide a kind of therapy, allowing an individual who is in some cultural conflict to live for a time in an easier fantasy world whose expressive models evade the actual world that troubles him.

Roberts and Sutton-Smith offer exciting insights as they specify which games teach people and which games assuage feelings of conflict. Roberts finds that there are three important kinds of games, each model-

[5] See J. M. Roberts and B. Sutton-Smith, "Child Training and Game Involvement," *Ethnology* 1, no. 2 (April 1962).

ing different activities and providing the players an opportunity to practice *different styles,* or *attitudes,* toward competition:

1. games of *physical* skill—based on a footrace model of particular cultural activities like chasing a runaway sheep or running away from a policeman—permit rehearsal of the attitude of hope for success by the exercise of speed and power

2. games of *strategy,* such as poker or Monopoly, model the activities of the market place and of management, and provide rehearsal of the attitude of hope for success by the exercise of clever decision making

3. games of *chance,* such as roulette or bingo, provide the hope for success by luck.

Examples of folk tales that involve these expressive models are 1) stories about Hercules for physical skill, 2) Aesop's tale of "The Clever Crow" for strategy, and 3) the story of Cinderella for chance.

We can schematize the causal assumption of Roberts and Sutton-Smith by a diagram relating the sociocultural level to the social-psychological one, as in Figure C:

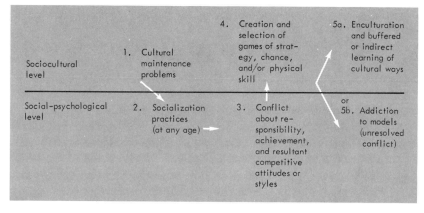

FIGURE C

Like McClelland's theory, the theory on which Figure C is based is quite difficult to test. Roberts and Sutton-Smith, however, have systematically tested the implications that each arrow of the figure represents. Let us look at a few of their tests.

One of the first tests had to do with the general relationship between items 1 and 4 in the diagram. The hypothesis was that the games actually played in a culture would model some aspect of the maintenance problems of the society as a whole. The findings were consistent. Although games of strategy exist in complex primitive societies, they tend to be absent in primitive societies that lack political integration and social classes. This difference suggests that games of strategy are related to problems of controlling complex social systems. Games of chance are related to a culture's belief in the supernatural. Although the games of chance tend to be absent in societies that view gods and spirits as mainly malevolent, they are present where supernatural beings are believed to be benevolent more than half the time. Games of physical skill in turn, seem to be related to a complex of environmental factors that lead to a higher general level of activity so that they occur in greater numbers in temperate climates than in the tropics.

The theory demonstrated in Figure C suggests that the selection or creation of games at the sociocultural level is causally *mediated* by the presence or absence of certain psychological conflicts that arise from socialization practices. Here Roberts and Sutton-Smith are able to test the indirect implications of the theory both cross-culturally (where total societies are the unit of analysis) and intraculturally (where individuals or sex groupings are the unit of analysis). The cogency of their theory is strengthened by the following findings that relate items 3 and 4 in Figure C.

1. The selection of, or creation of, strategy games is linked with pressure for, and probably conflict over, *obedience* in socialization

2. Chance games are associated with *responsibility* training

3. Physical skill games crop up, or are preferred, where *achievement* pressures are high.

From a cross-cultural point of view, it is also noteworthy that where there are many kinds of games in a society there is strong anxiety over achievement performance. In short, a "game culture" provides opportunities for individuals to assuage anxiety about their achievement behavior (because winning or losing in the game has little if any outcome other than anxiety-reduction), while at the same time rehearsing the players in the very processes of competition.

We can only touch on the rich findings that have been collected around the theory behind Figure C. Roberts and Sutton-Smith report, for example, on a study of preference for games of a large number of American boys compared with girls. Considerable evidence from both cross-cultural and American sources shows that boys are given higher achievement training, whereas girls are given more obedience and responsibility training. American girls (as of a few years ago, at least) show a greater preference for games of strategy (such as "I've Got a Secret" or "Twenty Questions") and for games of chance (such as "Bingo," "Spin-the-Bottle"), while the boys prefer games of physical skill (such as bowling, horseshoes, racing) or games that involve both physical skill and strategy (marbles, wrestling, football).

The final set of arrows in Figure C represents the *effects* on people of playing games. Games can have the usual effect of teaching the players the activities and rules of the society under conditions of *buffered*, or reduced, intellectual and emotional scale (see item 5a), or they can have the effect of addicting some of the players, to the games, presumably because of the particularly strong psychological conflicts they entered the game with (see item 5b). Investigation on this last aspect of the theory has only begun, but preliminary work points up the probability that college students who are addicted to games of strategy, such as poker (even to the point of playing the game as much as forty hours a week), are laboring under a particularly strong set of conflicts about their positions in the social system.

Note that Roberts's theory of models is by no means limited to games. Among the many areas explored through this expanding approach is music, which Roberts views as an expressive cultural model of speech or, possibly, of social interaction in general. Following the logic of his theory, therefore, we may consider that those individuals who have been socialized into a state of conflict regarding talking, or those who, more broadly, are hung up over sending (and receiving) emotions and evaluation, will be most prone to listen deeply to music. Various kinds of music (with parts, voices, and instruments), provide such individuals with a model of talking and interaction that proceeds in a predictable and acceptable manner and which can be turned on or off at will. Roberts and Cecilia Ridgeway have begun work on this consideration by showing that people who are in personal conflict over talking and expressing emotion listen to music more frequently and are more involved while listening than people who are not in conflict.[6] Ridgeway has begun a series of laboratory experiments at Cornell that should further clarify the relation between music and personal conflict. Related to this work is the rich cross-cultural research of Alan Lomax on folk song styles.[7] Moreover, the work of Barbara Ayres has shown that the percentage of a society's songs that are in "regular rhythm" (in which accented beats occur at regularly spaced intervals throughout the song, as in 2/4, 4/4, or 6/8 time) positively related to the frequency with which infants are carried around by their mothers in those societies.[8] Perhaps music has even deeper ties to the effects of human socialization than we yet imagine.

[6] J. M. Roberts and C. Ridgeway, "Musical Involvement and Talking," *Anthropological Linguistics* 2, no. 8 (November 1969): 223–46.

[7] A. Lomax, *Folk Song Style and Culture*, American Association for the Advancement of Science Publication 88 (Washington, D.C.: AAAS, 1968).

[8] B. C. Ayres, "Effects of Infant Carrying Practices on Rhythm in Music," mimeographed (University of Massachusetts at Boston, 1971); see also her work in Lomax, *Folk Song Style and Culture*.

This theory of models has many practical ramifications, many of them as yet unstudied. There is enough evidence to suggest, however, that a theory that joins the sociocultural and social-psychological realms according to the relationships shown in Figure C is a fruitful way of thinking about the relationship of social psychology to large-scale cultural and sociological processes.

Other Sources of Personality and Culture

Our discussion of the relation of social psychology to economic development and to cultural models, although brief, does introduce some of the causal complexities that arise from the large question we asked at the opening of this chapter. However, we should not feel that all behavorial scientists think in the interdisciplinary fashion we have been emphasizing here. Many factors that determine social behavior are still profitably studied from a single-discipline perspective. It may always be profitable to study social-psychological processes by themselves, as most of this book attests.

Nor should we be led to think that the work of Roberts and McClelland covers all the possible sources of personality or of culture. In order to dispel any such illusion let us look briefly at three studies that show the probable importance of (a) climate as a source of culture and personality, (b) religious beliefs as causes of personality training, and (c) personality factors in determining the structure of work groups.

John W. M. Whiting, a Harvard behavioral scientist, has shown with cross-cultural evidence that circumcision rites for boys are related to, and possibly causally involved with, the cultural occurrence of

(a) exclusive mother-infant sleeping arrangements (the child sleeps with the mother for several years until another baby or the father turns him out)

(b) a long postpartum sex taboo (sexual intercourse between parents is forbidden for some time following childbirth)

(c) patrilocal residence (newlyweds reside near the man's family).[9]

Whiting has emphasized that the circumcision rites are possibly a means of breaking the strong emotional bond of identification of the boys with their mothers, which developed in the long period of exclusive attention received by the boys and which leaves the boy confused as to his sexual identity.

Whiting shows empirically that patrilocal residence is often found

[9] J. W. M. Whiting, "Effects of Climate Upon Certain Cultural Practices," in *Explorations in Cultural Anthropology*, ed. Ward Goodenough (New York: McGraw-Hill, 1964), pp. 511–44.

where polygyny is practiced, and it is in these polygynous societies that the prolonged postpartum sex taboo is found. In turn, the sex taboo is related—and to Whiting, anchored causally—to a protein deficiency in the diet of the region (usually in tropical climates). Where mother's milk is the main source of protein for the infant, the mother must avoid becoming pregnant so that her milk will remain rich in protein. The sex taboo, therefore, helps the newborn child avoid *kwashiorkor*, the protein deficiency disease so tragically prevalent in these hot and humid areas.

The causal sequence goes like this: Because of a low protein diet, a long postpartum sex taboo is practiced to protect the baby from dietary deficiency if the mother gets pregnant again. Because this taboo leads men to look for other women, polygyny arises. Polygyny, in turn, leads to patrilocal residence patterns because the husband's relatives who surround the wives help keep them in line.

Finally, Whiting shows empirically that the exclusive mother-child sleeping arrangements tend to occur where hot summer temperatures encourage husbands and wives to sleep apart. In other words, various basic cultural phenomena—sex taboos, residence patterns, sleeping arrangements, polygyny, and circumcision rites—may all turn out to be, in part at least, clearly determined adjustments to some basic climatic and dietary conditions.

We should note that Frank Young sprang empirically and theoretically to the defense of those who wish to consider only sociocultural issues. Providing a stimulating and fruitful dispute with Whiting regarding many of these relationships, Young considered that the deep structure of male chauvinism in some cultures was merely a cultural spinoff of more basic factors.[10] This debate is a good example of the fruitfulness of scientific disagreement.

In vast contrast to climate as being a factor of cultural causation, let us consider the causation possibilities of ideas. We must not underestimate the power of ideas as causes of both personality and culture. An example can be found in a study by William Lambert, Leigh Triandis, and Margery Wolf on the correlates of beliefs that supernatural beings are benevolent or malevolent.[11] The study shows that in societies that conceive of the deities as being preponderantly malevolent—causing trouble, calamities, illness, and death—most of these cultural religious

[10] F. W. Young, "The Function of Male Initiation Ceremonies: A Cross-Cultural Test of an Alternative Hypothesis," *American Journal of Sociology* 57, no. 4 (January 1962): 379–91. In the same issue, see following "Comment," by J. W. M. Whiting (pp. 391–94) and "Rejoinder," by F. W. Young (pp. 394–96).

[11] W. W. Lambert, L. M. Triandis, and M. Wolf, "Some Correlates of Beliefs in the Malevolence and Benevolence of Supernatural Beings: A Cross-Societal Study," *Journal of Abnormal and Social Psychology* 58, no. 2 (1959).

beliefs can be sensibly viewed as reflections of the usual treatment received by a member of the society during early socialization. For example, the children in these societies receive more painful experiences at the hands of their otherwise affectionate parents than do children in societies where the deities are seen as preponderantly kind, and parents in such societies generally make a great use of punishment in rearing children.

One aspect of the story is not easy to understand, however. These usually punishing parents go out of their way to reward their children for self-reliant and independent behavior. The simplest explanation of the paradox appears to be that, imbued as they are with the notion that the world is a trap in which even the spirits are malevolent, these parents go out of their way to reward their children for self-reliant and independent behavior that would prepare them for surviving in a tough world.

In short, although the experiences in childhood of pain and punishment seem to explain why both parents and children would come to expect harm from the powerful deities, we can best explain the parents' behavior in rewarding self-reliance and independence because of their religious *beliefs*. No apparent outstanding climatic or geographic features have been discovered to explain why these particular behaviors are rewarded in children. Socialization practices color the religious beliefs, the religious beliefs in turn determine some of the child-training practices, and this cultural pattern helps determine personality. So goes the interpretation and Figure A will have to be made more complicated to handle it.

Joel Aronoff believes that the basic outlines of figures A, B, and C are *all* too simplified and do not give sufficient primacy to psychological events—such as those below the line of Figure A. He provides a fascinating account of the history of changes in cane-cutting gangs on a West Indies island.[12] His data show (and here we greatly simplify) that the work groups of the sugar-cane cutters changed over a period of a few years from an authoritarian structure that was based on the men's fear of the powerful and grasping foreman to a democratic structure where the foreman was weaker and where each man got paid for his own contribution. This change to a democratic structure occurred partly because a turnover of personnel produced a new type of person. The model cane cutter who used to be hung up by his need for social and economic safety now was a person who had developed "higher" motives (in Maslow's hierarchy), such as the need for self-esteem. There were fewer of the safety-oriented type of people because the conditions of

[12] J. Aronoff, *Psychological Needs and Cultural Systems* (New York: Van Nostrand Reinhold, 1967).

socialization had improved so that the cane cutters enjoyed stabilized family and community relationships. Mothers and fathers stayed home rather than go to other islands for jobs. Health care saved the lives of siblings and even adults. In general, as the family had fewer fears of personal disasters, wage earners were able to go beyond fear for psychological safety to considerations of self-esteem.

This increase in the worker's self-esteem forced a change in the very structure of the work group to make it possible for this new psychological need to be expressed and gratified. Aronoff would want to change our diagrams to recognize that psychological factors that *start* the social change process are on an equal footing with sociocultural factors (including certain environmental determinants). In his picture, then, there is an interchange between the sociocultural and psychological factors, and out of this come new personalities and new social structures. In terms of Figure A, Aronoff would want us to represent the process with reciprocating arrows between the processes above and below the line. We look forward to the further results of Aronoff's work as he takes the problems into the laboratory (as he has done) and then back out into the field. He may well be discovering some of the social and psychological conditions necessary for developing and maintaining democratic structures.

Aronoff and Ridgeway turn to experiments to more firmly grasp some of the causal sequences involved in these large theories, just as Roberts and Whiting move from a cross-cultural to an intracultural study to control for the different cultural contexts so as to be sure that certain processes are actually social-psychological. Two additional strategies of great interest must be mentioned.

Raoul Naroll, an anthropologist at the State University of New York at Buffalo, believes that we must develop repeated cross-cultural measures in order to grasp causal principles at the macrocosmic level. He points out that there is a strong cross-cultural correlation between the complexity of a civilization and its restrictions on premarital sex.[13] To greatly simplify, there are three theories of the causal influence of sexual behavior. One theory, using a sociocultural approach, suggests that the rise of a civilization causes structural social changes that lead to sexual restriction (particularly of females) so that the property can be controlled by controlling the women.[14] A second theory sees the causal factor being premarital sex restrictions, which increase creativity, which

[13] R. Naroll, "Causal Analysis of Holocultural Survey Data," mimeographed (prepared for the 1971 meeting of the American Psychological Association).
[14] J. Goody, I. Barrie, and N. Tahany, "Causal Inferences Concerning Inheritance and Property," *Human Relations* 24, no. 4 (August 1971): 295–314.

in turn, leads to a rise in civilization.[15] The third theory sees premarital sex restrictions as a more specific contributing factor in the development of large states.[16] Naroll proposes that if we can get repeated evidence that cultures with premarital sex restrictions have later become more complex, then we can begin to spot which factor is the more probable causal factor.

Harry Triandis would certainly agree with Naroll's suggestion, although his particular contribution (an example of which we saw in Chapter 3) has been to recognize that most sociocultural systems can be reflected in the thoughts, values, and expectations of its individuals. He (and others) have named these qualities *subjective culture* and have developed many social-psychological indexes for measuring these structures as seen by the individuals involved.[17] This approach, which brings the larger sociocultural events into direct relation with individuals (and groups), may serve all the behavioral sciences (sociology, anthropology, psychology, social-psychology) in uncovering the important mysteries of this general realm where personality is seen as both a cause and an effect of society and culture.

But these new methods and new visions are only now emerging from a time when these relationships have largely been seen (as they still are) as a question of whether the chicken or the egg came first. In the coming years we may break through to a generally agreed-upon causal picture; we may not. But the restlessness of the search and the intricacy of the problems are not new. They are captured rather well in this equally restless but hopeful passage, written by Confucius around 500 B.C.:

> The ancients who wished to illustrate the highest virtue throughout the empire first ordered well their own states. Wishing to order well their states, they first regulated their families. Wishing to regulate their families, they first cultivated their own selves. Wishing to cultivate their own selves they first rectified their hearts. Wishing to rectify their hearts, they first sought to be sincere in their thoughts. Wishing to be sincere in their thoughts, they first extended to the utmost their knowledge. Such extension of knowledge lay in the investigation of things.
>
> Things being investigated, knowledge became complete. Their

---

[15] J. Unwin, *Sex and Culture* (London: Oxford University Press, 1934).

[16] Y. Cohen, "Ends and Means in Political Control: State Organization and the Punishment of Adultery, Incest, and the Violation of Celibacy," *American Anthropologist* 71 (1969): 658–87.

[17] H. Triandis et al., *The Analysis of Subjective Culture*, New York: John Wiley, 1971.

knowledge being complete, their thoughts were sincere. Their thoughts being sincere, their hearts were then rectified. Their hearts being rectified, their own selves were cultivated. Their own selves being cultivated, their families were regulated. Their families being regulated, their states were rightly governed. Their states being rightly governed, the whole empire was made tranquil and happy.

Selected Readings

Chapter 1

ALLPORT, G. W. The historical background of modern social psychology. In *The handbook of social psychology*, vol. 1, ed. G. Lindzey and E. Aronson. 2d ed. Reading, Mass.: Addison-Wesley, 1968.

BURNHAM, J. C. Historical background for the study of personality. In *Handbook of personality theory and research*, ed. E. F. Borgatta and W. W. Lambert. Chicago: Rand McNally, 1968.

HOLLANDER, E. P., and HUNT, R. G., *Classic contributions to social psychology*. New York: Oxford University Press, 1972.

LAZARUS, R. S. *Personality*. 2d ed. Englewood Cliffs, N.J.: Prentice-Hall, 1971.

Chapter 2

GOSLIN, D. A., ed. *Handbook of socialization theory and research*. Chicago: Rand McNally, 1969.

LAMBERT, W. W., and WEISBROD, R. *Comparative perspectives on social psychology*. Boston: Little, Brown, 1971.

SEARS, R. R.; RAU, L.; and ALPERT, R. *Identification and child rearing,* Stanford, Calif.: Stanford University Press, 1965.

WHITING, B., ed. *Six cultures: Studies of child rearing.* New York: John Wiley, 1963.

ZIGLER, E., and CHILD, I. L. Socialization. In *The handbook of social psychology,* vol. 3, ed. G. Lindzey and E. Aronson. 2d ed. Reading, Mass.: Addison-Wesley, 1968.

Chapter 3

COLE, M.; GAY, J.; GLICK, J. A.; and SHARP, D. W. *The cultural context of learning and thinking.* New York: Basic Books, 1971.

HASTORF, A. H.; SCHNEIDER, D. J.; and POLEFKA, J. *Person perception.* Reading, Mass.: Addison-Wesley, 1970.

HOCHBERG, J. E. *Perception.* Englewood Cliffs, N.J.: Prentice-Hall, 1964. (Revised edition in preparation.)

KELLEY, H. H. *Attribution in social interaction.* New York: General Learning Corp., 1971.

TRIANDIS, H. *The analysis of subjective culture.* New York: John Wiley, 1972.

Chapter 4

BROWN, R. Models of attitude change. In *New directions in psychology,* ed. R. Brown et al. New York: Holt, Rinehart & Winston, 1962.

CAMPBELL, D. Social attitudes and other behavioral dispositions. In *Psychology, a study of a science,* vol. 6, ed. S. Koch. New York McGraw-Hill, 1963.

EDWARDS, A. L. *Techniques of attitude scale construction.* New York: Appleton-Century-Crofts, 1957.

FISHBEIN, M., ed. *Readings in attitude theory and measurement.* New York: John Wiley, 1967.

MC GUIRE, W. The nature of attitudes and attitude change. In *Handbook of Social Psychology,* ed. G. Lindzey and E. Aronson. 2d ed. Reading, Mass.: Addison-Wesley, 1969.

TRIANDIS, H. *Attitude and attitude change.* New York: John Wiley, 1971.

ZAJONC, R. B. Cognitive theories in social psychology. In *Handbook of Social Psychology,* vol. 1, ed. G. Lindzey and E. Aronson. 2d ed. Reading, Mass.: Addison-Wesley, 1969.

Chapter 5

BALES, R. F. *Personality and interpersonal behavior.* New York: Holt, Rinehart & Winston, 1970.

HEIDER, F. *The psychology of interpersonal relations.* New York: John Wiley, 1958.

KELLEY, H. H., and THIBAUT, J. W. Group problem solving. In *Handbook of Social Psychology*, vol. 4, ed. G. Lindzey and E. Aronson. 2d ed. Reading, Mass.: Addison-Wesley, 1969.

NEWCOMB, T. M. *The acquaintance process.* New York: Holt, Rinehart & Winston, 1961.

THIBAUT, J., and KELLEY, H. *The social psychology of groups.* New York: John Wiley, 1959.

SKINNER, B. F. *Science and human behavior.* New York: Macmillan, 1953.

Chapter 6

ASCH, S. E. *Social Psychology.* Englewood Cliffs, N.J.: Prentice-Hall, 1952.

FIEDLER, F. *Leadership.* New York: General Learning Corp., 1971.

JONES, E. E., and GERARD, H. B. *Foundations of social psychology.* New York: John Wiley, 1967. (Revised edition in preparation.)

KIESLER, C. A., and KIESLER, S. B. *Conformity.* Reading, Mass.: Addison-Wesley, 1969.

SHERIF, M., and SHERIF, CAROLYN W. *Social psychology.* New York: Harper & Row, 1969.

WALKER, E. L., and HEYNS, R. W. *An anatomy for conformity.* Englewood Cliffs, N.J.: Prentice-Hall, 1962.

WEICK, K. E. *The social psychology of organizing.* Reading, Mass.: Addison-Wesley, 1969.

Chapter 7

ARONOFF, J. *Psychological needs and cultural systems.* New York: Van Nostrand Reinhold, 1967.

FROMM, E., and MACCOBY, M. *Social character in a Mexican village.* Englewood Cliffs, N.J.: Prentice-Hall, 1970.

MCCLLELAND, D. C. *Motivational trends in society.* New York: General Learning Corp., 1971.

MINTURN, L. et al. *Mothers of six cultures.* New York: John Wiley, 1964.

WALLACE, A. F. C. *Culture and personality.* 2d ed. New York: Random House, 1970.

WHITING, J. W. M., and CHILD, I. *Child training and personality.* New Haven, Conn. Yale University Press, 1954.

Index

Tagiuri, Renato, 57
Tannenbaum, P. H., 93, 94n
Taylor, Donald, 67
Thematic Apperception Test, 38
Thibaut, John, 53–55, 106–7
Toman, Walter, 37
Triandis, Harry, 49, 66–88, 163
Triandis, Leigh, 18n, 160
Tucker, Richard, 70
Tunisia, 11–12

Volstead Act, 149

Wapner, S., 130
Weick, Karl E., 112, 139
Weisbrod, Rita, 19n

Whiting, Beatrice, 18n, 19, 30
Whiting, John W. M., 19, 29–30, 159–60
Winterbottom, Marian R., 38
Wolf, Arthur, 49
Wolf, Margery, 160
Wolfe, Thomas, 105–6
Woodworth, Robert, 48–49
Wright, Herbert F., 15–16

Young, Frank, 160

Zavalloni, M., 126
Ziller, R. C., 112
Zimbardo, P., 91